PENSIONS, SOCIAL SECURITY, AND
THE PRIVATIZATION OF RISK

*The Columbia University Press and Social Science Research Council
Series on the Privatization of Risk*

THE COLUMBIA UNIVERSITY PRESS AND SOCIAL SCIENCE RESEARCH COUNCIL SERIES ON THE PRIVATIZATION OF RISK

Edited by Craig Calhoun and Jacob S. Hacker

The early twenty-first century is witnessing a concerted effort to privatize risk—to shift responsibility for the management or mitigation of key risks onto private-sector organizations or directly onto individuals. This series uses social science research to analyze this issue in depth. Each volume presents a concise review of a particular topic from the perspective of the public and private allocation of risk and responsibility and offers analysis and empirical, evidence-based opinion from leading scholars in the fields of economics, political science, sociology, anthropology, and law. Support for the series comes from the John D. and Catherine T. MacArthur Foundation.

Jacob S. Hacker, ed., *Health at Risk: America's Ailing Health System—and How to Heal It*

Andrew Lakoff, ed., *Disaster and the Politics of Intervention*

Donald W. Light, ed., *The Risks of Prescription Drugs*

Katherine S. Newman, ed., *Laid Off, Laid Low: Political and Economic Consequences of Employment Insecurity*

Robert E. Wright, ed., *Bailouts: Public Money, Private Profit*

Pensions, Social Security, and the Privatization of Risk

EDITED BY MITCHELL A. ORENSTEIN

COLUMBIA UNIVERSITY PRESS | NEW YORK

A COLUMBIA/SSRC BOOK

COLUMBIA UNIVERSITY PRESS
Publishers Since 1893
New York   Chichester, West Sussex

Library of Congress Cataloging-in-Publication Data

Pensions, Social Security, and the privatization of risk /
[edited by] Mitchell A. Orenstein.
      p. cm. — (The Columbia University Press
and Social Science Research Council series on the
privatization of risk)
   ISBN 978-0-231-14694-4 (cloth : alk. paper) —
ISBN 978-0-231-14695-1 (pbk. : alk. paper) —
ISBN 978-0-231-51927-4 (ebook)
   1. Old age pensions — United States. 2. Pension
trusts — United States. 3. Social security — United States.
4. Privatization — United States. I. Orenstein, Mitchell A.
(Mitchell Alexander) II. Title. III. Series.

HD7105.35.U6P475 2009
331.25'20973 — dc22

                          2009003833

Columbia University Press books are printed
on permanent and durable acid-free paper. This
book is printed on paper with recycled content.
Printed in the United States of America

c 10 9 8 7 6 5 4 3 2 1
p 10 9 8 7 6 5 4 3 2 1

References to Internet Web sites (URLs) were
accurate at the time of writing. Neither the editor
nor Columbia University Press is responsible
for URLs that may have expired or changed since
the manuscript was prepared.

Design by Julie Fry
Cover by Vin Dang

CONTENTS

PENSIONS, SOCIAL SECURITY, AND
THE PRIVATIZATION OF RISK

Introduction

MITCHELL A. ORENSTEIN

The 2008 financial market crisis pushed pension reform to the top of the policy agenda in Washington, DC. Without substantial reform, Social Security benefits are expected to decline gradually over the coming decades, from 40% of the average worker's wage in 2002 to around 30% in 2030 (see Munnell in this volume). The result is that people's retirements are becoming more insecure. Financial turmoil has reduced confidence in the United States' workplace pension systems as well. Since the 1980s, employers who used to provide generous retirement pensions have backed away from that promise and switched to 401(k)-type pension savings accounts. In the 2008 crisis, 401(k) and individual retirement account (IRA) balances dropped sharply. Calculations presented in this book show that for nearly half of all retirees, reduced government and employer pensions will mean a scaled-down retirement with inadequate benefits. Younger people and those with lower incomes are the most vulnerable. If you have picked up this book, you may be worried about the future of your own pension — and rightly so. America's pension system needs to be fixed. This book puts forward solutions from leading experts that will help define policy debate in the years ahead. It is presented in clear language and intended to help nonspecialists formulate their own ideas about pension reform.

As the events of 2008 made clear, reforming the U.S. pension system means more than just fixing Social Security. Any approach must be two-pronged. It must address both future imbalances in the Social Security program and weaknesses in the workplace and individual retirement systems on which an increasing proportion of Americans now are forced to rely. The chapters in this book show why and how.

In weighing these problems, this book draws lessons for the United States from the experiences of other developed countries. While the U.S. pension system is unusual in some ways, many of the difficulties we face are similar to those of other countries, such as an aging population, declining Social Security benefits, and strained employer-based systems. A number of countries have been forced to confront these issues, but they have done so in different ways. Many developing countries and a few developed ones, like the United Kingdom and Sweden, have cut or "carved out" part of their Social Security systems in order to fund individual pension savings accounts. This is what President George W. Bush proposed for the United States in 2005. Other countries, such as Australia, Denmark, the Netherlands, New Zealand, and Switzerland, have mandated enrollment in a workplace pension for nearly all employees. The United Kingdom is considering similar action. These two routes to reform contain important lessons for the United States as it confronts its own pension system challenges.

THE CONTEXT OF U.S. PENSION SYSTEM REFORM

In order to correct the problems of the U.S. pension system, it is first important to put them in their particular context. The U.S. pension system is unique in at least two ways. First, the U.S. Social Security program provides lower benefits and costs less as a proportion of gross domestic product than similar programs in other wealthy countries. For instance, the United States spends 4.4% of total economic output on its Social Security program, while Germany, another major economy, spends 12.5%—about 2.8 times as much.[1] The relatively small size of the U.S. Social Security program is both a problem and an advantage for reform. It is a problem because low benefits leave Americans vulnerable to falling into poverty if Social Security declines even a little bit. It is an advantage because the relative cost of the program—and the cost of fixing it—is lower, putting a solution for reforming our pension system well within reach.

A second unusual feature of the U.S. pension system follows from the first. Since Social Security benefits are low, the United States has a long tradition of relying on supplemental workplace and individual pensions: one-third of all Americans currently depend on workplace pensions in addition to Social Security for part of their retirement income, and in recent years, IRAs have come to play a growing role. Our reliance on workplace and individual pensions also presents both an advantage and a problem for reform. It is an advantage because supplemental pensions offer more options for coping with the current crisis. It is a problem because as more and more people are forced to rely on them, workplace and individual pension systems are proving increasingly inadequate. They do not and will not provide enough benefits to enough people to compensate for the likely declines in Social Security. Yet these systems will be hard to change, given the complicated political interests of beneficiaries and providers.

While the U.S. pension system is somewhat unique, the causes of our present pension crisis are not. They are the same as those faced, to varying degrees, in countries around the world. First, the United States is getting older. An aging population strains pension system finances since a shrinking proportion of workers must pay for the retirement of a larger and larger proportion of retirees. Second, the politics of Social Security reform are difficult. Retirees and near-retirees and their representatives resist changes, even if it means shifting the burden onto the young. Many people are naturally suspicious of cuts in Social Security. At the same time, they do not want to pay more to preserve the benefits they (or their parents) currently have. The first step for pension reform is to address growing problems in Social Security. A second step is to transform the employer-based pension systems that have failed to guarantee Americans' retirement income security.

TACKLING SOCIAL SECURITY REFORM

Since President George W. Bush's efforts to cut back Social Security in 2005 in favor of a system of individual pension savings accounts, a consensus has grown on how to repair the endangered program. The Bush administration's approach to solving the problems of Social Security failed to persuade most Americans. With Social Security facing future shortfalls, cutting back the program is not a logical response since it does not address the problem of benefit adequacy. When Social Security falls into deficit in the coming decades because of the retirement of the baby boom generation and eventually exhausts the reserves of the Social Security Trust Fund, policymakers will be forced to reduce benefits. Since Social Security benefits are low to start with, many older Americans will fall into poverty. Protecting benefits requires one or more of these unpopular measures: increasing the retirement age, increasing the cap on Social Security income, or increasing the payroll tax rate.

The most effective way to solve the problems of Social Security would be to increase the statutory retirement age, as President Ronald Reagan did with considerable bipartisan support in a major 1983 reform. Under that reform package, the retirement age was increased from 65 to 67 over a twenty-two-year period starting in 2000. This, coupled with a payroll tax increase, enabled the United States to build up a Social Security Trust Fund to pay for the retirement of the baby boom generation and has kept the program solvent to this day. The United States needs to consider accelerating the pace of the phased increase in the statutory retirement age and further increasing it past 67 at some point in the future. Although an increase in the retirement age means an across-the-board cut in benefits, Americans are living longer. The average life expectancy at retirement is now above 80 for men and 85 for women. A growing proportion of Americans live beyond 95, spending thirty of those years in retirement. As Americans spend a longer period of their lives in retirement, retirement systems face an extraordinary burden. The statutory retirement age needs to be corrected for increases in life expectancy in order to keep Social Security solvent.

Another key element of Social Security reform would be to raise the cap on Social Security income. Social Security is paid for by a 12.4% payroll tax split equally between employers and employees. However, the amount of income subject to Social Security tax is capped. In 2008, workers paid Social Security taxes on the first $102,000 of their income. Under the Bush administration, the Social Security income cap was not raised in line with inflation or wage increases. The burden of the program has therefore fallen more and more on the middle class. A higher wage cap would provide a large part of the funds required to keep Social Security solvent and paying adequate benefits in the years ahead.

A third option to protect Social Security benefits would be to increase the Social Security payroll tax. Policymakers are likely to exhaust other options before increasing the payroll tax rate because of the political and economic problems with raising taxes. Policymakers could address the linkage between Medicare and Social Security benefits. Under current law, Medicare Part B premiums are deducted from Social Security checks, and the amount of that deduction is projected to rise sharply. Reforming the health care system would have a substantial influence on the future of Social Security.

As the United States gets closer to running through the Social Security Trust Fund, the government will be forced to act to ensure the adequacy of Social Security benefits. The sooner this happens, the better. The solutions are relatively clear. What is required is the political will to fix the program.

REWORKING WORKPLACE AND INDIVIDUAL PENSIONS

Social Security reform alone is not enough to resolve the U.S. pension crisis. While the program has provided sufficient income to keep older Americans out of poverty, it replaces on average 40% of pre-retirement income, an insufficient level to maintain a prior standard of living. Most Americans need to supplement their Social Security benefits with another source of retirement income. The most popular source has been an employer (or workplace) pension. However, America's workplace pension system also has proven inadequate. Only one-third of Americans are covered by an employer system, and the shift to 401(k)-type accounts has placed the retirement income of many at risk (see Burtless in this volume). The average head of household nearing retirement has only $60,000 in his or her 401(k) (see Munnell in this volume). As the first generation of workers covered by these plans retires, their inadequacy will become more glaring.

The Bush administration dramatically increased tax incentives for 401(k) and individual retirement accounts by raising the maximum contribution to individual pension savings accounts from $10,500 in 2000 to $15,500 in 2008. However, most of the gains went to relatively well-off citizens who contribute the maximum to these accounts (see Ghilarducci in this volume). The incentives provide nothing to the more than half of all workers who do not contribute. In this way, the U.S. government has spent substantial new funds subsidizing the retirement pension accounts of those who arguably need the money the least.

There are also problems with the regulation of these individual pension savings accounts. Individuals have been given a lot of choice over how much to contribute, how to invest, and how to use retirement savings. The trouble is that people have very often made bad choices — investing too little for retirement, investing it poorly, and cashing out too soon. As a result, most people who hold 401(k) accounts have very small balances, too small to provide an adequate retirement income.

Jacob Hacker has labeled the trend towards individual pension savings accounts part of a "great risk shift" or a privatization of risk that places mounting financial burdens on individuals rather than government or employers.[2] While enhancing individual choice, this approach has magnified retirement insecurity. Without significant changes to the way workplace and individual pension systems are managed and regulated in the United States, this country will not be able to meet its most pressing retirement challenges.

A SIMILAR STARTING POINT, DIFFERENT SOLUTIONS

The authors of this book share a similar perspective on the problems of the U.S. pension system. They are concerned first of all with benefit adequacy — making the U.S. Social Security program and workplace and individual pension systems more reliable as a source of retirement income for all. These authors, leading experts in their fields, believe that any pension reform should not cut but enhance an increasingly inadequate Social Security program in order to protect Americans from declining benefits in the years ahead. They object to the Bush administration approach, which was to carve out Social Security in order to encourage private pension savings accounts. They also share the view that Social Security reform by itself will not be enough. Any pension reform must also target the employer-based and individual pension systems that provide a growing share of U.S. retirement income.

The authors present different perspectives on how to achieve these objectives. Together, their chapters offer a stimulating overview of the main pension reform issues confronting the United States and the main policy options moving forward. A final chapter discusses the politics of reform and shows which international models are the most relevant to the United States. While representing the state of the art of policy discourse in Washington, DC and beyond, all the chapters have been written with an educated, nonspecialist audience in mind.

ADDRESSING THE PRIVATIZATION OF RISK

One of the key issues differentiating the chapters in this book is their approach to the privatization of risk. How and how much should people be protected from the risks inherent in individual pension savings accounts? Studies suggest that individuals often benefit from regulations that limit or discourage bad decision making. For instance, it turns out that more people will save for the future when they are automatically enrolled in a pension savings program, even when they have the opportunity to opt out. While a smaller proportion of people will sign up voluntarily, the vast majority will stay in such a program if auto-enrolled.

This undermines the idea that giving someone free choice enables that person to make the best personal choices. Pension decisions are so complex that most people faced with them are prone to confusion. Confronting a confusing choice, people do what is natural—delay or defer making a decision rather than making the one they are most comfortable with. Such delays and defaults can be costly. For this reason, many experts believe that individuals should be protected from the risk of making bad decisions about their pension savings. Protection from risk can be achieved in numerous ways.

Teresa Ghilarducci suggests a unique approach to limiting risk in individual pension savings accounts. In her proposal, individuals would invest money in a fund with a guaranteed rate of return: 3% above inflation. A government agency would manage the fund (or subcontract management to private companies). In order to smooth out investment risk, the government would use revenue from good years to subsidize the returns in bad years.

Gary Burtless bases his proposal instead on the existing 401(k) pension system. He argues that the risk of poor investment returns in individual accounts is less of a problem than the risk of not contributing to an individual pension savings account at all. He proposes to increase the proportion of employees enrolled in a workplace or individual pension from less than 50% to close to 100% by requiring all employers to auto-enroll their employees.

Alicia Munnell advocates creating a new tier of pension savings accounts that would supplant the 401(k) system, which she argues has systematically failed to help people accumulate sufficient retirement savings. She is also concerned that the 401(k) system will further fail people at retirement by providing poor choices for retirement income. She advocates creating a new, mandatory individual account system from scratch, without being bound by 401(k) politics and regulations.

Each of these author proposals would reduce retirement risk considerably, but in different ways and to differing degrees.

REFORM OR REPLACE?

In addition to differing on how to address the privatization of risk, the experts in this book take different approaches on whether to reform or replace the existing workplace and individual pension systems. Teresa Ghilarducci recommends scrapping the tax advantages of the current systems and replacing them with a new system subsidized by those funds. She believes that by applying the tax breaks from the 401(k) system to the new system, it would pay for itself without new taxes. It would also be much fairer since the current 401(k) system subsidizes primarily the well-to-do. Alicia Munnell proposes building a new pension system as well, one that would consist of privately managed individual pension savings accounts. This would be created on top of the existing pension system and thus compete with the 401(k) system, if not replace it. Gary Burtless instead proposes to build upon the current system; rather than replacing it with something different, he proposes extending it to all employees and changing its regulations. This also would make the tax breaks the system provides more equitable.

In addition to commonsense Social Security reforms, these proposals represent three distinct options for reform of the U.S. pension system. Together, they reflect a significant advance on the Bush administration approach and represent a step forward toward ensuring America's retirement security in the years ahead.

A further chapter by Gary Burtless addresses the instability in individual account balances caused by financial market turbulence. Burtless shows that while a portfolio of 100% stocks outperforms portfolios invested in bonds on average, the value of a 100% stock portfolio fluctuates wildly. In the best years, retirees can expect a lifetime of 4% contributions to replace more than 80% of pre-retirement income; in 2008 that figure was closer to 20%. A combined stock-bond portfolio reduces uncertainty about retirement income considerably but produces a considerably lower average return.

A final chapter shows how the experiences of other countries can be brought to bear on the reform debate in the United States. While the U.S. pension system has its own distinctive history and politics, lessons from other countries help to illuminate America's unique path. Through a review of international experience, this chapter shows that the United States needs to look at countries, such as Australia, New Zealand, and the United Kingdom, that have transformed or are transforming their workplace pension systems to make participation and/or enrollment mandatory. This route to reform both fits with the culture and size of our Social Security system and is politically feasible.

The U.S. pension system is faced with major challenges, but by drawing on its own expertise and other countries' experiences, the United States has the opportunity and ability to ensure an adequate retirement income for generations yet to come.

NOTES

Acknowledgments: The editor would like to thank Elizabeth Isaman of Johns Hopkins University SAIS for her outstanding research assistance and Paul Price and Debra Yoo of the Social Science Research Council for their expert editorial contributions.

1   Axel H. Börsch-Supan and Christina B. Wilke, "The German Public Pension System: How it Was, How it Will Be," WP 2003-041 (working paper, University of Michigan Retirement Research Center, March 2003).

2   Jacob S. Hacker, *The Great Risk Shift: The Assault on American Jobs, Families, Health Care, and Retirement and How You Can Fight Back* (Oxford: Oxford University Press, 2006).

CHAPTER ONE

Retirements at Risk

ALICIA H. MUNNELL

That retirement is becoming increasingly at risk should come as no surprise. The press is filled with calls to fix Social Security, shore up employer pensions, and make 401(k) plans work better. Indeed, Social Security benefits — relative to earnings — are declining. Employer pensions have become increasingly scarce. And 401(k) balances are generally inadequate. Moreover, the recent financial crisis caused balances in 401(k) plans and individual retirement accounts (IRAs), which consist largely of rollovers from 401(k) plans, to decline by almost $2 trillion from October 9, 2007, the peak of the market, to October 9, 2008. At the same time that the retirement system is contracting, longevity is steadily rising. People are going to have to rely increasingly on their own efforts to accumulate retirement assets for a very long period of retirement.

This chapter is structured as follows. The first section explains why saving is so hard for most people. The second section describes how employer pensions and Social Security helped solve the problem by making saving automatic and how both these sources are now declining in importance. The third section quantifies the impact of the contracting retirement system on future households, showing that 44% will not be able to maintain their pre-retirement standard of living. That percentage rises to about 60% once health care outlays are included explicitly. The fourth section then explores what can be done. Working longer is an obvious alternative, but easier said than done. Making the existing retirement system work as well as possible is a priority. This involves securing Social Security by increasing revenues to avoid additional benefit cuts and improving the drawdown options for 401(k) plans. But these changes alone are likely to prove inadequate, and people are going to need an additional tier of retirement saving. That tier should probably be funded rather than on a pay-as-you-go basis and should incorporate the best attributes of defined benefit plans, such as uniform participation, pooled investments, and benefits paid as annuities. The final section draws conclusions about the future of retirement in the United States.

SAVING FOR RETIREMENT IS HARD

During the preindustrial period, the individual typically did not need help to save for retirement, because the elderly generally continued to work for as long as they could. They took on less taxing jobs as their strength or acuity declined and stopped working only when no longer able. Well into the nineteenth century, three of four elderly Americans still worked.[1] The elderly in preindustrial economies also often owned property that provided an income. Family farms and handicraft businesses were natural vehicles for accumulating wealth as part of a worker's normal routine, and many elderly were able to retire from active labor by selling or leasing these assets. The minority of the elderly who could no longer work and had little or no property would often rely on their children or local community for economic support.

Two developments — urbanization and industrialization — transformed the economics of aging. Urbanization concentrated the population in the large labor and product markets, which undermined the traditional sources of family or communal assistance. Industrialization transferred production from the household to larger and more rationally organized enterprises. The outcome was an enormously productive economy. But it also undermined the ability of the elderly to support themselves through work or the ownership of income-producing assets. Industrialization separated the process of gaining a livelihood from the process of acquiring income-producing property. To build up such assets, industrial workers had to consciously set aside a portion of their earnings and invest those funds.

The saving and investing process is hard. It requires a good deal of foresight, discipline, and skill. Economists' life-cycle model of saving is based on the assumption that people have the knowledge to forecast their needs decades in the future and then the discipline and skill to act on those forecasts. To properly forecast retirement needs and annual saving requirements, people need to predict their earnings over their lifetime, how long they will be able to work, how much they will earn on their assets, how much they will need in retirement, and their life expectancy. Recent surveys suggest that—even today—people are not very good at planning for retirement. In 2008, only 18% of respondents indicated that they were very confident that they had put aside enough for retirement, 28% had not saved anything for retirement, and 53% had not even tried to figure out how much they might need.[2]

The current work in behavioral finance, which brings together economics, finance, and psychology, has tried to identify some of the factors that lead to poor preparation for retirement. Not surprisingly, one problem is myopia—people are absorbed in their daily routines, or prefer not to think of their own old age, and fail to see what lies in the future. A second problem is the low value many people seem to place on their future well-being. One explanation offered by psychologists and economists is that people are "hyperbolic" discounters, in that their near-term discount rates are much higher than their long-term discount rates.[3] In the case of saving, a dollar put aside today is seen as growing fast in the short run but slowly thereafter, so benefits more than a short period away have very little value. In old age, of course, such people would say they consumed far too much and saved far too little when young.

A third issue is self-control.[4] That is, many people say they should be saving for retirement but find it very difficult to act on that knowledge. Researchers find that making decisions about retirement is one area where workers are likely to procrastinate. In fact, one common response of workers as to why they do not participate in savings plans is, "I never get around to it." Some reasons that people never get around to it are obvious: a secure retirement tomorrow involves sacrificing consumption today; postponing the start of saving has no immediate penalty; and the process is complicated. The psychology literature has documented the tendency for individuals to put off making decisions as the complexity of tasks increases.[5]

Because of myopia and lack of discipline, workers often need commitment devices to ensure that they put money aside.[6] In response, every industrial nation, not just the United States, has created retirement income programs sponsored by the national government and employers.

THE EXPANSION AND DECLINE
OF RETIREMENT INCOME SYSTEMS

Employer pensions evolved over the course of the nineteenth century, and Social Security was enacted in the mid 1930s. By the 1960s, the two together produced a secure retirement for many workers.[7] The heyday did not last for long, however. By the early 1980s, both public and private programs were set on a declining trajectory.

EMPLOYERS STEP UP TO THE PLATE

Large U.S. employers, which came to have large numbers of permanent employees, introduced pensions as instruments for shaping their relationship with their workforce. Pensions helped develop career employees and managers, to whom large employers increasingly delegated authority to oversee their operations. Pensions paid a comfortable benefit, pegged to salary and years of service, to those white-collar workers who remained with the employer until the specified retirement age. Workers who left early typically got only a return of their own contributions. The pension thus functioned as an incentive to remain with the organization, do good work, and rise in the ranks.

Pensions also proved valuable in shaping relationships with blue-collar workers. Organizations in industries such as railroads, urban transit, and manufacturing employed very large numbers of blue-collar workers to operate their capital-intensive, high-throughput operations. These employers typically paid high market wages to attract better workers, win their loyalty, and fend off unions. But beyond a certain point, employers found it more effective to provide "industrial insurance" rather than ever-higher wages. This insurance protected workers and their families against the loss of earnings due to accident, death, illness, and aging.

Finally, by the end of the nineteenth century, many large employers saw their offices, machine shops, and locomotives increasingly staffed by older workers whose productive abilities had clearly declined. So, beginning at the turn of the century, large employers in the United States began to mandate retirement at a specified age. To remove older workers without damaging relations with the rest of the workforce, or the public at large, they retired these workers on pension.[8]

By the end of the 1930s, employer pension plans had become standard in mature big businesses. They were critical personnel tools for strengthening, then severing, relationships with workers. And they were a critical source of support for the 15% of the workforce lucky enough to have such coverage.

Although World War II consumed many of the nation's resources that might have been directed toward improved provisions for old age, pensions expanded as an unintended consequence of wartime wage controls. Restricted from raising wages, many employers competed for scarce workers by offering generous pensions. Moreover, the era's high income tax rates made pensions an attractive vehicle for sheltering income.

In the immediate postwar period, employees focused on cash wages to recover ground lost during the period of wartime stabilization. The main expansion of today's pension system actually began during the 1950s. The drivers of that expansion were threefold. First, pension plans had become an essential component of corporate personnel systems, so coverage grew as corporate big business blossomed.[9] Second, the special tax treatment of employer pensions became significantly more valuable in the face of mass income taxation.[10] And third, unions, which had gained powerful collective bargaining rights in 1949, made pensions a standard component of labor agreements throughout the unionized sector in the decade that followed.[11]

Employer participation in the provision of old-age income had firmly taken root by the mid 1960s. These employer pensions were defined benefit plans, which provide benefits in the form of a lifetime payment based on years of service and salary. These plans require workers to make almost no important financial choices for retirement. The firm enrolls all eligible workers, makes contributions, and makes investment decisions (or retains professional investment managers), generally providing a lifetime benefit at retirement. The worker's only real choice is when to collect benefits. These employer-sponsored defined benefit plans — in combination with Social Security — provided long-service workers a secure and comfortable retirement.

The system was far from perfect, however. Only half the workforce was covered by the supplementary employer plans at any moment in time. And benefits were not indexed for inflation after retirement, so beneficiaries could see the purchasing power of their pension dwindle in the face of rising prices. Moreover, the bankruptcy of Studebaker in 1963, which left 4,100 workers with just 15% of their promised benefits, highlighted a gaping hole in the pension system. Pensions could disappear if the company had not put aside enough money to pre-fund them.

After more than ten years of hearings and prolonged debate, Congress passed the Employee Retirement Income Security Act (ERISA) in 1974.[12] ERISA succeeded in strengthening employees' claims on benefits, but the costs associated with its vesting, funding, and insurance provisions may also have encouraged employers to move away from defined benefit plans.

EMPLOYERS BACK AWAY

Beginning in the early 1980s, the types of pensions provided by employers began to change. Pension coverage shifted from traditional defined benefit plans to 401(k) plans, which are essentially savings accounts. When 401(k) plans began to spread rapidly in the early 1980s, they were viewed mainly as supplements to employer-funded pension and profit-sharing plans. Since 401(k) participants were presumed to have their basic retirement income security needs covered by an employer-funded plan and Social Security, they were given substantial discretion over 401(k) choices, including whether to participate, how much to contribute, how to invest, and when and in what form to withdraw the funds.

Over the past twenty-five years, however, the private pension landscape has changed dramatically. Most workers covered by an employer plan now have a 401(k) as their primary or only plan (see figure 1.1). Yet 401(k)s still operate under the old rules. Workers continue to have almost complete discretion over whether and how much to contribute, how to invest, and how and when to withdraw their funds.

In theory workers could accumulate substantial pension wealth under 401(k) plans. But *in practice* they have not. The evidence indicates that a significant fraction of participants make serious mistakes at every step along the way. A quarter of those eligible to participate choose not to do so. Almost half fail to diversify their investments. Many over-invest in company stock. Almost no participants re-balance their portfolios as they age or in response to market returns. Most importantly, many cash out when they change jobs. The result has been that the balances in these accounts are very low. According to the Federal Reserve Board's 2004 *Survey of Consumer Finances,* the typical head of a household with such an account who was approaching retirement had accumulated only about $60,000.[13] Moreover, whatever modest balances people had accumulated in their 401(k) plans and IRAs were crushed by the 42% decline in equity values between October 9, 2007, and October 9, 2008.

But the real challenge lies ahead. When people get to retirement, they will receive their balances as lump sums. They will have to figure out how they want to spread that money over their retirement years. It is a very difficult task. People have no idea how long they will live, and, with the increases in longevity, one third of women and 20% of men will live into their nineties. So the baby boom generation will face an enormous challenge.

THE EXPANSION AND CONTRACTION OF SOCIAL SECURITY

At the same time that employers are withdrawing from bearing the risks of their employees' retirement saving, the government's social insurance program is also contracting. The United States created its Social Security program in 1935, in the midst of the Great Depression. It was one of the last industrialized countries to do so. The elderly nevertheless remained a distinctly poor population. The 1950 Social Security Amendments substantially expanded coverage and restored benefits that had been seriously eroded by inflation during the war, but replacement rates — benefits relative to pre-retirement earnings — remained at 30% for the model average worker.

In 1972, Congress sharply increased Social Security benefits to roughly a 40% earnings replacement rate for the benchmark average earner. Today, Social Security is the backbone of the retirement income system. As shown in figure 1.2, households in the bottom third of the older population get 85% of their income from Social Security; those in the middle third, 69%; and those in the top third, 36%.

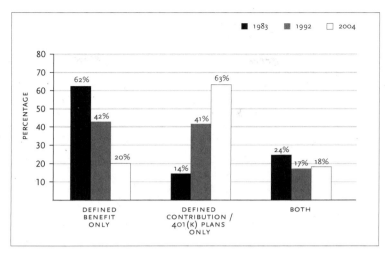

Figure 1.1   Percent of workers with pension coverage by type of plan from survey of consumer finances, 1983–2004   [Source: Alicia H. Munnell and Annika Sundén, "401(k) Plans Are Still Coming Up Short," *Issue in Brief* (Center for Retirement Research at Boston College) 43 (March 2006).]

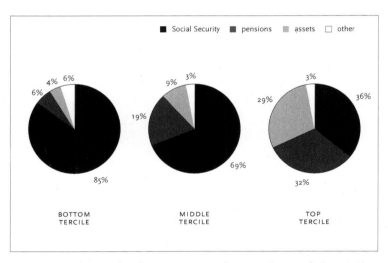

Figure 1.2   Social Security benefits as a percentage of non-earned income for households aged 65 and over, Current Population Survey 2006   [Source: U.S. Bureau of Labor Statistics and U.S. Bureau of the Census, *Current Population Survey* (Washington, DC, 2007).]

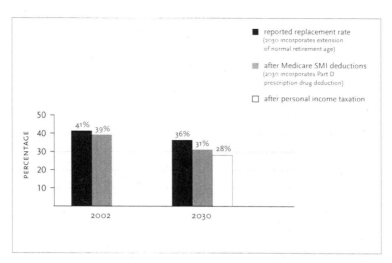

Figure 1.3   Social Security replacement rates for the medium earner, 2002 and 2030
[Source: Author's calculations based on Alicia H. Munnell, "The Declining Role of Social Security," *Just the Facts* (Center for Retirement Research at Boston College) 6 (February 2003).]

Soon after Social Security's expansion, however, it became clear that the cost of pay-as-you-go government plans would dramatically rise in the future. Rapid population aging would require a drastic increase in payroll tax rates to finance benefits. Moreover, the program faced a short-term funding crisis. In response, the National Commission on Social Security Reform, headed by Alan Greenspan, presented a series of reforms that would enable the system to pay immediate benefits and supposedly restore solvency over the seventy-five-year horizon. Their report, issued in January 1983, became the basis for the 1983 Social Security Amendments.

One component of the 1983 reform package that will have important implications going forward is the extension of the Full Retirement Age from 65 to 67. Today, the hypothetical "medium earner" retiring at age 65 receives benefits equal to about 41% of previous earnings. After paying the Medicare Part B premium, which is automatically deducted from Social Security benefits before the check goes in the mail, the replacement rate is 39%. But, under current law, Social Security replacement rates are scheduled to decline for three reasons (see figure 1.3). First, the increase in the Full Retirement Age is equivalent to an across-the-board cut.[14] Second, Medicare Part B premiums and premiums for the new

Part D drug benefit are slated to increase sharply due to rising health care costs.[15] Finally, Social Security benefits will be taxed more under the personal income tax, as the exemption amounts are not indexed to inflation. As shown in figure 1.3, these three factors alone will reduce the *net* replacement rate for the medium worker, who claims at age 65, from 39% in 2002 to 28% in 2030. Note that this figure does not include any additional benefit cuts that might be enacted to shore up the solvency of the Social Security program.[16]

In summary, the shift to 401(k) plans and the contraction of Social Security mean that individuals will be required to take on more of the responsibility for providing their own retirement income. And the 401(k) plan experiment has shown that they are not very good at this task. What lies ahead for future households?

QUANTIFYING THE FUTURE OUTLOOK

To quantify the effects of shifting the risk and responsibility of providing retirement income to the individual, the Center for Retirement Research at Boston College constructed the National Retirement Risk Index (NRRI). The NRRI shows the percentage of working-age American households who are "at risk" of being financially unprepared for retirement. The 2004 Index calculates a replacement rate for each household in the *2004 Survey of Consumer Finances* — projected retirement income relative to pre-retirement earnings — and compares that replacement rate with a benchmark that is defined as adequate (see figure 1.4). Those who fail to come within 10% of the benchmark are defined as being at risk.

The NRRI shows that, even if people retire at age 65 and households annuitize all their wealth including the receipts from reverse mortgages on their homes, 44% will not be able to maintain their standard of living in retirement. An analysis by age group indicates that the situation gets more serious over time (see figure 1.5). About 35% of the Early Boomers (those born between 1948 and 1954) will not have an adequate retirement income. This share increases to 44% for the Late Boomers (those born between 1955 and 1964) and then rises to 48% for the Generation Xers (those born between 1965 and 1974).[17] This pattern of increasing risk reflects the retirement income issues discussed above as well as the fact that people are living longer.

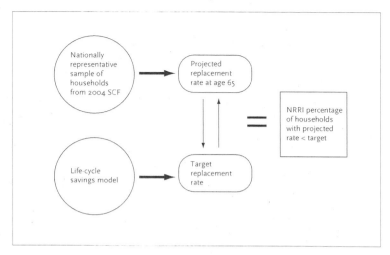

Figure 1.4 National Retirement Risk Index [Source: Author's illustration.]

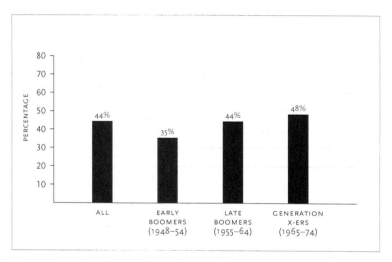

Figure 1.5 National Retirement Risk Index by birth cohort [Source: Alicia H. Munnell, Mauricio Soto, Anthony Webb, Francesca Golub-Sass, and Dan Muldoon, "Health Care Costs Drive Up the National Retirement Risk Index," *Issue in Brief* (Center for Retirement Research at Boston College) 8-3 (February 2008).]

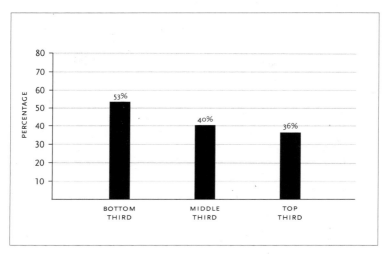

Figure 1.6 National Retirement Risk Index by income group, 2004 [Source: Center for Retirement Research at Boston College, *Retirements at Risk: A New National Retirement Risk Index* (Chestnut Hill, MA, 2006).]

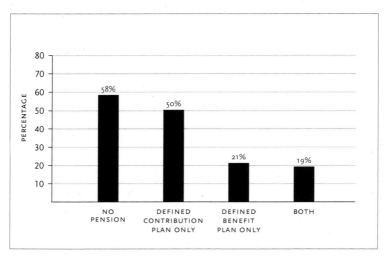

Figure 1.7 National Retirement Risk Index by pension coverage, 2004 [Source: Center for Retirement Research at Boston College, *Retirements at Risk: A New National Retirement Risk Index* (Chestnut Hill, MA, 2006).]

The pattern of risk by income class and pension coverage is just what one would expect (see figures 1.6 and 1.7). For those in the bottom third, 53% will be at risk; this outcome compares to 36% for those in the highest third. Similarly, those without pensions fare much more poorly than those with pension coverage. The pattern by income group reflects the fact that those in the bottom third rely almost exclusively on Social Security benefits that are scheduled to decline sharply relative to pre-retirement income.[18] But it is interesting that a large share of households in the middle and top thirds of the income distribution are also at risk. Of course, the practical meaning of "at risk" differs by a household's level of income. At risk households in the lowest income group may have trouble affording life's basic necessities. In contrast, at risk households in the highest income group are not in danger of falling into poverty. However, they do face the prospect of a difficult adjustment that may require them to lower their retirement lifestyle expectations. And the median income for this group is $100,000, which means that many of these households are not particularly rich.

AND WHAT ABOUT HEALTH CARE EXPENSES?

In addition to shifting risk for retirement income to the individual, employers have cut back on their provision of post-retirement health care benefits. This development means that again households will be at risk. Between 1988 and 2008, the percentage of large firms offering post-retirement health care benefits dropped from 66% to 31% (see figure 1.8). The decline in participating firms actually understates the extent of the cutback because the generosity of the benefits has also been reduced. In response to the rising costs of health care, employers have increased retiree contributions to premiums, increased retiree coinsurance or co-payments, raised deductibles, and increased out-of-pocket limits.[19] Moreover, many of those providing post-retirement health benefits today have terminated such benefits for new retirees.

The at risk numbers discussed previously do not explicitly identify health care spending. The implicit assumption is that spending on health care is a substitute for other forms of consumption. This assumption implies that retired households can rearrange their basket of consumption — consuming more health care and less of other goods — and still maintain their standard of living. An alternative — and probably more realistic—way to treat retiree health care expenses is as a "tax" that people have to pay in retirement. Viewing health care from this perspective, the household's goal then becomes one of maintaining its non-health care consumption in retirement. In this scenario, households will be at risk if they do not have enough resources to maintain non-health care pre-retirement consumption.

Explicitly including health care raises the percentage of households at risk—that is, not capable of maintaining their pre-retirement standard of non-health care consumption—from 44% to 61% (see figure 1.9). Because health care costs are rising rapidly and the income system is contracting, a much larger percentage of later cohorts will be at risk. The NRRI rises from 50% for Early Boomers to 68% for Generation Xers.

WHAT CAN BE DONE?

Without change, modest 401(k) balances and reduced Social Security replacement rates are almost sure to prove inadequate in retirement.

ONE ANSWER: WORKING LONGER

Working longer is an obvious solution. People are not going to be able to continue to retire at 62 and maintain their pre-retirement living standards over an increasingly long period of retirement. Working longer is a powerful response because it produces three benefits. First, each additional year in the workforce increases income directly through earnings from work and investments. Second, working longer increases social insurance benefits actuarially by 7% to 8% per year. And third, it reduces the number of years over which retirement savings need to be spread. The implications for retirement saving are striking. Delaying retirement from age 62 to age 70 would cut required retirement assets by almost 80% (see figure 1.10).[20]

The problem is that getting everyone to work longer is not simple.[21] It requires thought and planning on the part of individuals. It also requires employers to retain, train, and even hire older workers. These are huge hurdles to overcome. Moreover, working beyond age 62 may not be possible for almost a third of the population because of health or employment problems. Therefore, new institutions and products are needed to improve saving and provide for orderly decumulation once

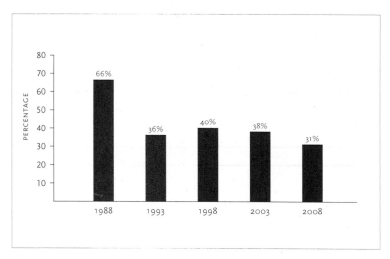

Figure 1.8   Percentage of employers offering retiree health benefits (large firms with 200+ workers), 1988–2008   [Source: The Kaiser Family Foundation and The Health Research and Educational Trust, *Employer Health Benefits: 2008 Annual Survey* (KFF/HRET, 2008), http://ehbs.kff.org/pdf/7790.pdf.]

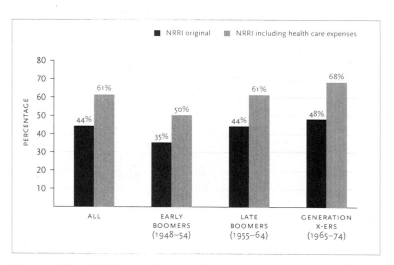

Figure 1.9   Effect of health care on the National Retirement Risk Index, 2006
[Source: Alicia H. Munnell, Mauricio Soto, Anthony Webb, Francesca Golub-Sass, and Dan Muldoon, "Health Care Costs Drive Up the National Retirement Risk Index," *Issue in Brief* (Center for Retirement Research at Boston College) 8-3 (February 2008).]

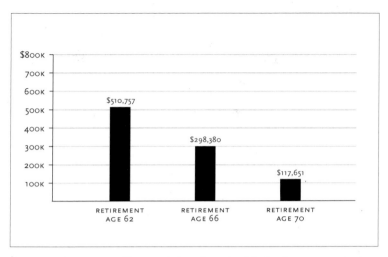

Figure 1.10   Assets required for a married couple earning $58,560 after taxes to maintain 80% of after-tax pre-retirement income, 2004   [Source: Congressional Budget Office, "Retirement Age and the Need for Saving," *Economic and Budget Issue Brief* (Washington, DC, May 2004).]

people reach retirement. The goal is to provide people, after a lifetime of work, with a stream of retirement income that is adequate, reliable, and protected against inflation.

STABILIZE SOCIAL SECURITY

The most immediate need is to stabilize the U.S. pay-as-you-go social insurance program. With the demise of private sector defined benefit plans, this program will soon become the only source of automatically annutized benefits in the retirement income system for the majority of American workers. It is also the only source of inflation-adjusted retirement income. This system pools risks both across the population and across cohorts. The recent financial crisis has highlighted the importance of a stable source of retirement income that older Americans can rely on.[22]

As discussed earlier, the U.S. Social Security program is already contracting. Replacement rates will decline as the Full Retirement Age increases from 65 to 67, as Medicare premiums take a bigger chunk out of benefits, and as un-indexed thresholds in the personal income tax cause

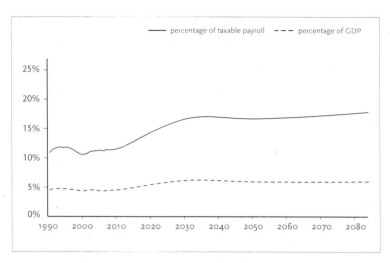

Figure 1.11   Social Security costs as a percentage of gross domestic product and taxable
payroll, 1990–2085   [Source: Board of Trustees of OASDI, *The 2008 Annual Report of the Board of Trustees of the Federal
Old-Age, Survivors and Disability Insurance Trust Funds* (Washington, DC: Social Security Administration, 2008).]

taxation to move further down the income distribution. It seems difficult to
reverse the causes of this contraction: proposals generally involve increasing the Full Retirement Age, not reducing it; health care reform appears
focused on increasing coverage, not on constraining cost; and today's large
deficits will require raising taxes in the future, not lowering them. However, making additional cuts in benefits to offset the program's long-term
financing shortfall would leave many people with little base of support.

   Therefore, the program requires more revenues. Over the next
seventy-five years, Social Security's long-run deficit is projected to
equal 1.7% of covered payroll earnings. The easiest way to interpret the
meaning of the seventy-five-year deficit is in terms of the size of the tax
increase required to restore solvency. That is, if the payroll tax rate were
raised immediately by roughly 1.7 percentage points — 0.85 percentage
point each for the employee and the employer — the government would
be able to pay, at least through 2082, the current package of benefits for
everyone who reaches retirement age.

   A lasting fix for Social Security would require additional changes.
Solutions that focus just on the next seventy-five years typically involve

the build-up of trust fund assets in the near term and the sale of those assets to pay benefits in the out years. Since the trust funds have no further bonds to sell in the seventy-sixth year, the program will fall suddenly short of money. Lasting solvency would require either a pay-as-you-go system with substantially higher payroll tax rates or the build-up of a trust fund larger than that required for seventy-five-year solvency, the returns from which could cover some of the costs.

The challenge of Social Security's shortfall looks considerably less daunting when Social Security outlays are projected as a percentage of Gross Domestic Product (GDP) rather than as a percentage of taxable payrolls (see figure 1.11). The cost of the program is projected to rise from 4.3% of GDP today to 6% of GDP in 2040 and to drop back to 5.8% by the end of the seventy-five-year projection period. Thus, additional revenues of about 1.5% of GDP would put the system on long-run balance.[23]

Tax increases are not painless. But since the benefits are modest, the increases in revenues required to close the financing gap are manageable. Stabilizing this important component of the retirement income structure is of the highest priority — and the sooner the better.

MAKE 401(K) PLANS WORK BETTER

After stabilizing Social Security, the second order of business is to make 401(k) plans work better. They need to be an easy and automatic way for people to save over their work life for retirement and to draw down assets in retirement. Some progress has been made. The Pension Protection Act of 2006 gave a big boost to automatic enrollment. Studies have shown that it is possible to dramatically increase participation rates by changing the default so that workers are enrolled automatically and must take affirmative action to opt out.[24]

One problem with automatic enrollment, however, is that the very inertia that makes the approach effective for participation can lock people into low contribution levels and conservative investments. That is, if the employer automatically enrolls people at, say, a 3% contribution and invests in a money market fund, five years later these very same people will still be contributing 3% into a money market fund. As a result, they will have accumulated very little. To avoid such outcomes, the 2006 legislation also encourages automatic increases in the default rates and sanctions default investments with higher risks and returns.

In 2005, the Department of Labor issued regulations that should reduce the cashing out of small balances ($1,000–$5,000). Prior to the new regulations, almost 90% of participants cashed out small amounts when they left their company.[25] Experts agreed that one likely reason for the high cash-out rate was that a check, rather than a rollover, was the default. The employer is now required to roll over a small balance into an IRA, unless the separating employee elects to have it cashed out or rolled over into a 401(k) plan at his new company.

Now that legislation and regulation have addressed the biggest problems with the accumulation phase of 401(k) plans, the most significant remaining problem pertains to decumulation. That is, when employees receive their distribution as a lump sum at retirement, how will they allocate their retirement assets over an uncertain life span? They face the risk of either spending too rapidly and outliving their resources or spending too conservatively and consuming too little. These risks could be eliminated with the purchase of an annuity, but very few retirees buy annuities today. They are expensive for the average person because of administrative and marketing costs and adverse selection.[26] Married couples achieve some degree of risk sharing within the family. People may also want to hold onto their wealth for a bequest or in anticipation of large health-related expenses. Basically, too few individuals understand the risk of outliving their resources or appreciate the higher level of income that annuities offer. They instead view an annuity as a gamble with the insurance company, in which the company wins if they die early.

If the goal is to encourage annuitization, the annuity must be made as cheap, easy, and safe as possible. Voluntary individual annuities are riskier as well as costlier than defined benefit annuities.[27] Participants must now worry about when they purchase an annuity. Should they do it immediately upon retirement or later when they have a better sense of their health and income needs? Moreover, annuity payments are highly sensitive to interest rates, which means that different cohorts of retirees who annuitize will likely end up with different monthly benefits for the same total accumulations.[28] Under traditional defined benefit plans, workers were insulated from these fluctuations.[29]

Various government initiatives could help make the private provision of individual annuities less expensive, complex, and risky. Government could lower administrative costs if it could pool large numbers of participants. To the extent that lowering administrative costs increases participation, it would also reduce adverse selection and thereby further improve the payout per dollar of premium. The government is also the most likely entity to provide inflation-indexed annuities at a reasonable cost in a short period of time. Finally, the government is in a much better position than the individual to absorb interest rate risk. It could smooth out payments over time so that different cohorts do not end up with dramatically different benefits for the same accumulations.[30]

Even with the best federal government support, annuities may still seem unattractive to the average participant. Many people simply do not like giving up a pile of cash for a stream of income. An alternative approach is to make annuities the default in distributions from a 401(k) plan. This proposal is much more controversial than automatic enrollment. Experts agree that almost everyone is better off participating than not participating in a plan, but it is less clear that everyone is better off with an annuity. Moreover, it is much more difficult to unwind an annuity, since giving people their money back if, say, they got sick, would undermine the mortality pooling intrinsic to annuities. But some partial approach may be feasible. For example, make annuities the default for half the 401(k) balance and annuitize the amount slowly—say over five years—in order to allow people for whom annuities are not the right answer time to halt the process. The default annuity should be inflation adjusted and for married couples, a joint-and-survivor plan.[31] Again, participants could affirmatively change to a lump-sum payment, a nominal annuity, or a variable annuity.[32]

The important point is that, despite the progress to date in making 401(k)s more automatic, the decumulation phase looms as a potential disaster as baby boomers face the daunting challenge of allocating their 401(k) assets over their retirement span. The government must take some initiatives to increase the use of annuitization.

One final note: while attention has been focused on improving the performance of 401(k) plans, their relative importance has decreased in terms of total retirement assets. Yes, 401(k)s hold more assets than traditional defined benefit plans, but IRAs are now bigger than either defined benefit or defined contribution plans, and their performance is going to have a major impact on retirement security in the future (see figure 1.12). Preliminary data suggest that IRAs underperform employer-sponsored plans. IRAs are too big and important a form of retirement saving to not know what is going on with these accounts. Some mechanism is needed to identify the asset allocations in these accounts as well as to document the inflows and outflows. Only by including IRAs in the picture will it be possible to understand how well people are investing for retirement.

A NEW TIER OF RETIREMENT INCOME

Assume that all possible steps are taken to make the existing retirement saving mechanisms work as well as possible. 401(k) plans with automatic provisions boost participation and contributions. Retirees have attractive and efficient ways to draw down their financial and housing wealth. Individuals recognize the need to work longer and plan to extend their careers. Employers are open to retaining and hiring older workers because they believe that older workers will stay for a meaningful period of time and because they have the tools to retire those workers when they are no longer productive. Even in this optimistic scenario, it is very likely that people will not have enough income to maintain their living standards once they retire. One third of households will have nothing but Social Security, and Social Security replacement rates are scheduled to decline even under current law. The remainder will have 401(k) accounts, but the pressures to spend 401(k) balances on college costs and other pressing needs may continue to produce modest balances.

With a diminished Social Security program, uncertain 401(k) outcomes, and a third of households with no pensions at all, American workers are going to need an additional tier of government-supported retirement income (see figure 1.13). This is not a new idea. The Carter Commission on Pension Policy recommended in 1981 a mandatory universal pension system (MUPS). Under this proposal, every employer would contribute a minimum of 3% of payroll to a tax-deferred defined contribution pension plan.[33]

Over the past twenty-five years, however, we have learned a lot in terms of the design of retirement systems. First, some provision has to be made for low-income workers. It is reasonable to assume that the cost of such a mandatory savings program would be borne by workers, not their employers. Reducing wage growth in exchange for future retirement benefits is probably a reasonable trade-off for middle-income workers. But people with a lifetime of low wages are often not in a position to sacrifice current consumption for additional retirement income. Nor do

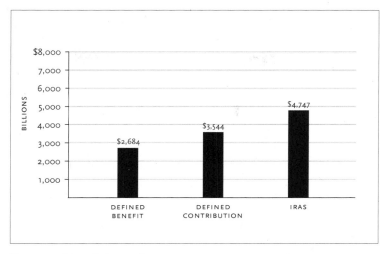

Figure 1.12   Private Retirement Assets, 2007   [Source: U.S. Board of Governors of the Federal Reserve System, *Flow of Funds Accounts of the United States* (Washington, DC, September 18, 2008).]

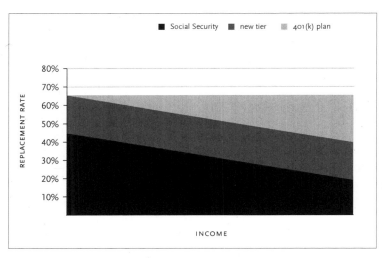

Figure 1.13   Additional tier of funded, privately managed retirement saving
[Source: Author's illustration.]

they derive benefits from the tax favors accorded such contributions, as they typically do not pay tax. Thus, benefits for low-income workers need to be subsidized.

Second, the 401(k) experiment has made it clear that certain features of defined benefit plans should be built into any additional tier. Participation should be universal, investments should be pooled to spread risk, and benefits should be paid in the form of annuities. American workers need to be insulated from the gut-wrenching swings in the stock market.

The purpose of this discussion is not to generate a particular recommendation. The point is that more retirement programs will most likely be needed, and an additional tier of government-supported retirement saving offers the flexibility of providing automatic credits for low-income workers without affecting their wages. At a minimum, given all that is known about the power of defaults, automatic participation with a potential to opt out might be the least controversial approach. The important message, however, is that more retirement saving will probably be necessary for people not to suffer a decline in their standard of living when they retire.

CONCLUSION

Employers have withdrawn from the provision of both income and health care benefits in retirement. Moreover, this withdrawal has occurred just as the task of accumulating adequate retirement income has gotten harder. The implication of these developments is that increasing numbers of future retirees will be unprepared for retirement. The National Retirement Risk Index indicates that 44% of today's households will not be able to maintain their living standards in retirement. The only way out of this dilemma is for people to stay in the workforce longer and acquire more retirement income. Neither goal can be accomplished without government initiatives.

Keeping people working longer will be very difficult to accomplish if Social Security continues to pay benefits beginning at age 62. Almost 60% of workers grab these benefits as soon as they become available, suggesting that they provide an incentive to retire early. The perception that workers will retire early also discourages employers from hiring, training, and promoting older employees since they are expected to be on the job for only a few additional years. Increasing the earliest eligibility age under Social Security would improve the incentives for older workers to remain in the labor force and for employers to hire them. Of course, increasing the early retirement age would require an expansion of other programs for the significant portion of the population for whom continued work is not a viable option.

Government is also key to making best use of the existing income programs. Although considerable progress has been made in automating 401(k) plans, the decumulation phase looms as an enormous problem as employees approach retirement with nothing but 401(k) balances. They face the risk of either spending too rapidly and outliving their resources or spending too conservatively and consuming too little. These risks could be eliminated with the purchase of annuities, but the annuity market in the United States is small. Government could improve the market for annuities in a number of ways and should consider introducing the annuity as the default in 401(k) plans. Government involvement is also essential to make it possible for people to tap their home equity in retirement.

Even if all the recommended changes occurred, however, Americans would need more institutions for retirement saving. These arrangements will not develop without the impetus of government. Repeated efforts to expand pension coverage have had virtually no impact. At any moment in time, less than half the private sector workforce is covered by a plan, the same percentage as in 1979, and even at retirement a third of households have never spent any time at a job with pension coverage. The United States should have an additional tier of retirement saving. This tier should be funded rather than pay-as-you-go and privately rather than publicly managed, although government needs to play a role to reduce the costs and risks. Moreover, low-income workers — who have seen virtually no increases in real wages over the last quarter century and derive no benefits from pension tax favors — will be hard pressed to defer more income to retirement and will need to be subsidized.

Finally, solving Social Security's financing problem should be framed in terms of life-cycle savings needs not as a budgetary hole that needs to be plugged. From this perspective, it is clear that we need to raise the revenue to maintain scheduled Social Security benefits.

NOTES

1   Much of the historical background comes out of conversations with or earlier work by Steven Sass, primarily Steven A. Sass, *The Promise of Private Pensions: The First Hundred Years* (Cambridge, MA: Harvard University Press, 1997). See also our joint work: Alicia H. Munnell and Steven A. Sass, *Working Longer: The Solution to the Retirement Income Challenge* (Washington, DC: Brookings Institution Press, 2008); and Alicia H. Munnell, Steven A. Sass, and Mauricio Soto, "Employer Attitudes toward Older Workers: Survey Results," *Work Opportunities Brief* (Center for Retirement Research at Boston College) 3 (July 2006).

2   Employee Benefit Research Institute, "The 2008 Retirement Confidence Survey: Americans Much More Worried About Retirement, Health Costs a Big Concern," *Issue Brief* (EBRI) 316 (April 2008). Similarly, in a survey of 10,000 workers in a single firm, 68% responded that their saving was too low; they should be saving 14% but were only saving 6%. See James Choi, David I. Laibson, Brigitte C. Madrian, and Andrew Metrick, "Defined Contribution Pensions: Plan Rules, Participant Decisions, and the Path of Least Resistance," W8655 (working paper, National Bureau of Economic Research, December 2001).

3   See David I. Laibson, Andrea Repetto, and Jeremy Tobacman, "Self-Control and Saving for Retirement," *Brookings Papers on Economic Activity* 1998, no. 1:91–196.

4   Richard H. Thaler and H. M. Shefrin, "An Economic Theory of Self-Control," *Journal of Political Economy* 89, no. 2 (1981): 392–406.

5   See, for example, Eldar Shafir and Amos Tversky, "Thinking Through Uncertainty: Nonconsequential Reasoning and Choice," *Cognitive Psychology* 24, no. 4 (October 1992): 449–74; and Sheena S. Iyengar and Mark R. Lepper, "When Choice is Demotivating: Can One Desire Too Much of a Good Thing?" *Journal of Personality and Social Psychology* 79, no. 6 (December 2000): 995–1006. A strong negative relationship between the number of funds offered in a 401(k) plan and the 401(k) participation rate is documented in the economic literature: having an additional ten funds in the plan menu reduces the participation rate by 1.5 to 2 percentage points. Sheena S. Iyengar, Wei Jiang, and Gur Huberman, "How Much Choice is Too Much?: Contributions to 401(k) Retirement Plans," PRC WP 2003-10 (working paper, Pension Research Council at the Wharton School, 2003).

6   See David I. Laibson, "Golden Eggs and Hyperbolic Discounting," *Quarterly Journal of Economics* 112, no. 2 (May 1997): 443–77. A recent commitment device is the "Save More Tomorrow" program. Under this plan, individuals who want to save more but indicate that they cannot do so now make a commitment to increase their contributions at some time in the future. See Shlomo Benartzi and Richard H.

Thaler, "Save More Tomorrow: Using Behavioral Economics to Increase Employee Saving," *Journal of Political Economy* 112, no. 1 (February 2004): s164–s187.

7   In the 1960s, about 35% of the private sector workforce was covered by an employer-sponsored pension, and an additional percentage picked up coverage at some point over their lifetimes. With a few exceptions, such as TIAA-CREF, most plans were defined benefit. Assuming the median replacement rate in the 1960s was roughly the same as in 1992, the first year of the Health and Retirement Study, then these plans would have raised the typical covered worker's total replacement rate to 55 to 60%—30 to 35% from Social Security and 20 to 25% from a defined benefit plan. For estimates of defined benefit replacement rates in 1992, see Olga Sorokina, Anthony Webb, and Dan Muldoon, "Pension Wealth and Income: 1992, 1998, and 2004," *Issue in Brief* (Center for Retirement Research at Boston College) 8-1 (January 2008).

8   See Sass, *The Promise of Private Pensions.*

9   The long big business boom was largely driven by giant mass-production, mass-distribution enterprises—in industries ranging from autos, steel, and consumer goods to telecommunications, banking and insurance, transport, and public utilities.

10   Favorable tax provisions had a limited effect on coverage before the war as less than 10% of the adult population typically paid tax. But the postwar growth of mass income taxation made pensions far less costly to employers and workers and encouraged their spread.

11   The big industrial unions won generous pension benefits in 1949 and 1950 as part of a political settlement that included long-term labor agreements, controls on labor militancy, and the passage of the 1950 Social Security Amendments.

12   ERISA's principal objective was to secure the rights of pension plan participants so that a greater proportion of covered workers would receive their accrued benefits. The legislation introduced participation and vesting standards to make it easier for workers to establish legal claims to benefits. Funding and fiduciary standards included in the law were to ensure that money would be available to pay the legal benefit claims. Despite the funding requirements, the possibility remained that some plans might terminate with inadequate assets. To protect plan participants against this contingency, ERISA also established the Pension Benefit Guaranty Corporation (PBGC), a mandatory insurance program that imposes premiums on defined benefit plans to insure workers against the loss of basic retirement benefits.

13   See Alicia H. Munnell and Annika Sundén, "401(k) Plans Are Still Coming Up Short," *Issue in Brief* (Center for Retirement Research at Boston College) 43 (March 2006).

14 Under legislation enacted in 1983, the increase in the Normal Retirement Age began with those born in 1938 (turning 62 in 2000) and will be fully phased in for those born in 1960 (turning 62 in 2022).

15 The premium for Medicare Part B is projected to increase from 9% of the average Social Security benefit in 2007 to 12% in 2030 (according to unpublished data from Centers for Medicare and Medicaid Services). See Centers for Medicare and Medicaid Services, *Annual Report of the Boards of Trustees of the Federal Hospital Insurance and Federal Supplementary Medical Insurance Trust Funds* (Washington, DC, 2008).

16 For married couples, and most Americans retire as part of a married couple, Social Security already replaces a significantly smaller share of household earnings than it did as recently as 1990 and will replace even less going forward. See Alicia H. Munnell, Geoffrey Sanzenbacher, and Mauricio Soto, "Working Wives Reduce Social Security Replacement Rates," *Issue in Brief* (Center for Retirement Research at Boston College) 7-15 (October 2007). The reason is the dramatic increase in the labor force participation of married women. As married households have increasingly relied on the earnings of working wives, these earnings have not produced a comparable increase in Social Security benefits because the program provides a guaranteed spousal benefit for the wife equal to 50% of her husband's Primary Insurance Amount—the benefit to which he would be entitled at the Full Retirement Age. The increased labor force participation of married women will increase the household's Social Security benefits only to the extent that benefits based on their earnings records exceed this spousal minimum. The average Social Security replacement rate for one-earner couples in the *Health and Retirement Study* is thus 58% compared to 41% for two-earner couples. See Alicia H. Munnell and Mauricio Soto, "How Much Pre-Retirement Income Does Social Security Replace?" *Issue in Brief* (Center for Retirement Research at Boston College) 36 (November 2005).

17 This sample does not include Generation Xers born after 1974.

18 For example, Social Security's Full Retirement Age (FRA) is scheduled to rise to 67. For all Early Boomers, the FRA is 66. For the Late Boomers, the FRA increases by two months per year starting for those born in 1955 until it reaches age 67 for those born in 1960. For all Generation Xers, the FRA is 67.

19 The Kaiser Family Foundation and Hewitt Associates, *Prospects for Retiree Health Benefits as Medicare Prescription Drug Coverage Begins: Findings from The Kaiser/Hewitt 2005 Survey on Retiree Health Benefits* (KFF/Hewitt, December 2005), http://www.kff.org/medicare/upload/7439.pdf.

20 The example in figure 1.10 sets a target retirement income of $47,000. At age

62, the couple gets $20,100 from Social Security, which provides 43% of this target amount. If the couple works to age 66, these benefits rise 38%, to $27,600, and provide 59% of the couple's target retirement income. If the couple works to age 70, these benefits rise an additional 38%, to $38,100, and provide 81% of the couple's target retirement income. The assets required are the amount the couple would need at retirement to purchase an annuity from the Federal Thrift Savings Plan to reach the target.

21 Munnell and Sass, *Working Longer: The Solution to the Retirement Income Challenge.*

22 For a discussion of the losses inside and outside of employer-sponsored pensions, see Alicia H. Munnell and Dan Muldoon, "Are Retirement Savings Too Exposed to Market Risk?" *Issue in Brief* (Center for Retirement Research at Boston College) 8-16 (October 2008).

23 To put the required increase in perspective, defense outlays declined from 5.2% of GDP in 1990 to 3% in 1999 and then rose to 4% in 2005, so the economy can easily weather swings of this magnitude. See Congressional Budget Office, *The Budget and Economic Outlook: Fiscal Years 2008–2018* (Washington, DC, 2008).

24 Brigitte C. Madrian and Dennis F. Shea, "The Power of Suggestion: Inertia in 401(k) Participation and Savings Behavior," *The Quarterly Journal of Economics* 116, no. 4 (November 2001): 1149–1187.

25 Alicia H. Munnell and James G. Lee, "Changing 401(k) Defaults on Cashing Out: Another Step in the Right Direction," *Just the Facts* (Center for Retirement Research at Boston College) 12 (September 2004).

26 For an analysis of why people may not buy annuities, see Jeffrey R. Brown and James M. Poterba, "Joint Life Annuities and Annuity Demand by Married Couples," *Journal of Risk and Insurance* 67, no. 4 (December 2000): 527–54; Jeffrey R. Brown, Olivia S. Mitchell, James M. Poterba, and Mark J. Warshawsky, *The Role of Annuity Markets in Financing Retirement* (Cambridge, MA: MIT Press, 2001); Laurence J. Kotlikoff and Avia Spivak, "The Family as an Incomplete Annuities Market," *Journal of Political Economy* 89, no. 2 (April 1981): 372–91; and Olivia Mitchell, James M. Poterba, and Mark J. Warshawsky, "New Evidence on the Money's Worth of Individual Annuities," w6002 (working paper, National Bureau of Economic Research, April 1997).

27 Individuals cannot purchase on their own the same annuity that they would have received under a traditional defined benefit plan. First, the voluntary nature of annuitization under a 401(k) plan creates a major adverse selection problem, which significantly increases the cost per dollar of annuity income. Second, administrative and marketing costs are significantly higher when annuities are purchased one

by one rather than in bulk. Third, the explosion of 401(k) plans greatly changed the relative price of annuities for women and men.

28 The variation is substantial. A $1,000 premium would have purchased a monthly income of $9.50 in 1989, when the yield on a ten-year Treasury note was about 8.5%; the monthly payment in March 2003 was about $6.69 per $1,000 as ten-year Treasury note yields fell below 4%.

29 One further issue that no one had to think about in the past is the safety of the insurance company. To date, few annuitants have taken a loss on fixed annuities, but it has happened. Two relatively large insurance companies ended up paying only seventy cents on the dollar after they got into trouble as a result of bad investments. The main purchasers of annuities to date, moreover, have been large sophisticated sponsors of defined benefit pension plans, not millions of relatively unsophisticated consumers. If individuals have to shop for annuities on their own, they will have to consider the health of the insurance company as well as all the other factors that play into the decision about allocating their 401(k) funds at retirement.

30 The government could take a number of approaches. The most aggressive would be to set up a government agency that received premiums from individuals, invested the money, and paid the monthly benefits. That is, the government would take on the full administrative, underwriting, and investment responsibilities. An alternative approach would be for the government to specify a standard type of annuity, perhaps including inflation indexing and a maximum load factor, and issue requests for proposals to private sector insurers. If the private insurance companies could satisfy these requirements, the government could serve as a clearinghouse and direct consumers to companies that offered these standard annuities. The government could also act as a purchaser or reinsurer of the approved annuity sold by private companies. The goal would be to establish a public-private partnership that provides 401(k) participants with the annuities they need at retirement.

31 The lesson learned from defined benefit plans is that employees otherwise fail to provide for their spouses. Husbands typically selected the single-life annuity, which pays higher monthly benefits. Wives, who typically outlive their husbands, then lose all pension income when their husband dies. The Employee Retirement Income Security Act of 1974 required that all pension plans that provide annuities automatically pay married couples in the form of a joint-and-survivor annuity. (The 1984 Retirement Equity Act amends this protection by requiring the spouse's notarized signature when the joint-and-survivor option is rejected.) Instituting the default significantly increased protection for wives. A joint-and-survivor annuity should also be the default option for married couples in defined contribution plans. Those who

want to opt out for a single-life annuity should be free to do so, with a signature from their spouse, as they are under current law for pension plans.

32 This proposal raises two issues. The first is the additional cost to 401(k) plans. Sponsors of these plans have always had the option to disburse benefits in the form of annuities, but they see providing annuities as more burdensome and costly than making lump-sum payments. Thus care must be taken to minimize the burden on plan sponsors so as not to endanger pension coverage. The second issue is that the private market for inflation-indexed annuities is nearly nonexistent. Since Treasury inflation-protected securities have been available in the United States since 1997, the explanation for the lack of indexed annuities must be lack of demand. If left on their own, individuals tend to select annuity options with the highest initial payment. But inertia is also a powerful force, and setting inflation-indexed annuities as the default would almost certainly increase demand.

33 All employees over age 25 with one year of service would participate; vesting would be immediate; and benefits would not be integrated with Social Security. Company MUPS plans would be managed as company plans are today—through pension trusts, insurance companies, and other financial institutions. If employers did not want to administer their own plans, they could send their contributions to a clearinghouse under the authority of the Social Security Administration to be invested in private capital markets. Those investments could be managed either by a private investment manager designated by the participant or by an independent board appointed by the president.

CHAPTER TWO

Expanding Participation in America's Workplace Retirement System

GARY BURTLESS

Most people who work for pay expect to stop working at some point. Under normal circumstances, that day arrives when a worker voluntarily leaves a final job and begins retirement. If misfortune strikes, workers may be forced to leave their jobs as a result of an involuntary layoff, or because they are too sick or incapacitated to continue working. Whatever the reason for their retirement, workers need a source of adequate income to replace the wages they earned while employed. Social Security is the cornerstone of retirement income for most Americans. Ninety percent of the population over the age of 65 receives Social Security, and monthly Old-Age and Survivors Insurance benefits account for 40% of their total cash incomes. Among the aged who are in the bottom one-fifth of the old-age income distribution, Social Security benefits account for almost nine-tenths of their total cash incomes.[1] Since the overwhelming majority of middle- and low-income retirees derive the bulk of their retirement incomes from Social Security, it is essential that these benefits be both predictable and protected against the effects of inflation.

For many middle- and high-income workers, however, a critical source of retirement income in addition to Social Security is a pension from an employer retirement plan. Employer pensions are important to workers who earn average and above-average pay because Social Security benefits replace less than half their pre-retirement wages. Unless Social Security pensions are increased substantially, which seems unlikely, employer pension plans should be expected to provide a sizeable share of the retirement income available to middle- and high-wage workers. Unfortunately, about half the private sector workers in the United States hold jobs that are not covered by an employer retirement plan. Uncovered workers can set aside part of their salary in an individual retirement account, outside the workplace retirement system, but that kind of saving requires planning, conscious sacrifice, and self-discipline. Some workers are up to the challenge, but many are not. It is easier for most of us to save when our employers automatically withhold part of each paycheck and invest it for us in a retirement account. If the funds are placed in an account from which we cannot make withdrawals until we retire, most of us will reach old age with a tidy nest egg.

Too few workers are offered automatic payroll withholding for retirement saving. In this chapter, I argue that all private employers should be required to offer their workers either traditional pensions or retirement savings accounts. Even if participation in such accounts remains voluntary, employees should be offered the option of automatic withholding for retirement saving. For workers who are at least 21 years old and not enrolled in a traditional pension plan, saving in retirement accounts should be offered as the default option. Workers could elect to reduce their payroll withholding below the default percentage, but unless newly hired workers specify a lower saving rate, they should be enrolled automatically in a plan that sets aside a minimum percentage of their wages in a sensible mix of stocks and bonds. Employers that do not want to manage retirement accounts for their employees should be offered the option of transferring that responsibility to a government-sponsored entity, whose obligations would include record keeping and the selection of private fund managers. The fund managers would in turn be responsible for investing workers' contributions.

In an environment of wide fluctuations in asset market prices, it may seem strange to urge the government to establish minimum standards for employer retirement savings plans. Workers who save steadily for retirement over a lengthy career may still reach old age with only a small nest egg if asset prices fall precipitously just before they reach their planned retirement age. In fact, that is precisely the situation faced by workers past age 60 who placed their savings in the stock market and hoped to retire in 2008. However, if workers and their employers make no provision at all for retirement saving, workers will face even bleaker prospects in old age. By itself, a Social Security pension does not replace even half the monthly paycheck earned by workers who are paid average or above-average wages. For the foreseeable future, middle-class Americans and their employers will be responsible for topping up the modest pensions most of us can expect from Social Security. Under these circumstances, it makes sense to require private employers to help their workers save for retirement, either through a traditional retirement plan or through regular payroll withholding in a 401(k)-style pension plan.

The remainder of this chapter describes the current workplace retirement system, assesses some of the risks that system poses to workers, and offers a reform agenda to mitigate those risks. Many critics of the current system focus on shortcomings of the 401(k) plans that employers have established in recent years. Many of these critics would like to resurrect the traditional pension plans that dominated the workplace before 1980. I argue that old-fashioned retirement plans posed risks of their own, though the risks differed from the ones common to newer types of plans. The main risk facing workers today is that they will not be covered at all by a workplace retirement plan. If they are enrolled in a purely voluntary plan, they face a considerable risk of under-saving for retirement. I argue for reforms that reduce those risks.

THE WORKPLACE RETIREMENT SYSTEM

Employer pensions come in two basic flavors. Traditional retirement plans offer defined benefit pensions. Employees who are enrolled in a defined benefit plan accumulate pension credits for each year they are employed and covered by the plan. An employee's eventual pension usually depends on the number of years of service under the plan and the worker's average wages during the last few years of employment with the firm. In most cases, the pension lasts for the remaining life of the retiree and possibly a surviving spouse. In a traditional defined benefit plan, the employer contributes enough money to finance the full cost of the plan. The employer also bears the financial risk of ensuring the pension fund contains enough reserves so that promised pensions can be paid in full even if the sponsoring company goes bankrupt.

The second kind of retirement plan offers defined contribution pensions. In this type of plan, employers and workers make regular contributions into a retirement investment account, with the contribution calculated as a percentage of each worker's monthly pay. Funds in a worker's account accumulate during years of covered employment, earning a rate of return that is determined by the allocation of funds into different types of investments and by the market returns on those investments. The allocation of pension investments might be determined by the employer, though it is nowadays more common for investments to be selected by individual workers from among a menu of investment options chosen by the employer. The most common type of defined contribution plan is a 401(k) plan, named after a provision in the U.S. income tax code. When workers leave their employer, they can leave their pension accumulation in the employer's defined contribution plan or withdraw it as a lump-sum payment. Some employers offer retirees the option of purchasing an annuity, which can provide a monthly income flow for the remainder of the worker's life and possibly that of a surviving spouse. It is more common, however, for retirees to roll their pension accumulation into an alternative, self-managed account, such as an individual retirement account (IRA). A crucial distinction between defined contribution plans and traditional defined benefit plans is that workers in a defined contribution plan bear the financial risk that their retirement savings might earn poor returns. If a worker makes bad or unlucky investment choices, the value of the pension accumulation at the point of retirement can be very low. In a traditional defined benefit plan, the financial risk of poor financial performance is borne by the employer sponsoring the plan rather than by the worker.

Over the past quarter century, the percentage of American workers covered by an employer pension plan has changed little, but the fraction who are offered traditional defined benefit pensions has fallen sharply. About half of all wage and salary workers are employed by a company or government agency that offers pension coverage to its workers, and about 40% of all employees participate in an employer-sponsored plan. Among workers on full-time work schedules, pension coverage and participation in a pension plan are higher. Slightly more than half of all full-time, year-round workers participate in an employer-sponsored retirement plan.[2] The U.S. Department of Labor collects annual informational returns about pension plans sponsored by private employers. The

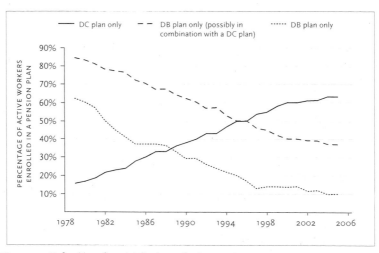

Figure 2.1   Defined benefit and defined contribution pension coverage among private sector workers covered by an employer-sponsored pension plan, 1979–2005   [Source: Employee Benefit Research Institute, "FAQs About Benefits - Retirement Issues," EBRI, http://www.ebri.org/publications/benfaq/index.cfm?fa=retfaq14 (accessed April 22, 2008).]

Labor Department's tabulation of these forms furnishes information about the types of pensions provided to private sector employees who are enrolled in company retirement plans. In 1979 almost 85% of pension-covered workers in the private sector were enrolled in a defined benefit plan, possibly in combination with a supplemental defined contribution plan. In that same year, 62% of pension-covered workers were enrolled solely in a defined benefit plan. Only 16% of pension-covered workers were enrolled solely in a defined contribution plan (see figure 2.1). By 2005 the percentages of private sector workers enrolled in the two kinds of plans were almost reversed. The fraction of pension-covered workers enrolled solely in a defined contribution plan had risen to 63%, while the fraction enrolled solely in a defined benefit plan had fallen to just 10%. Twenty-seven percent of pension-covered workers were enrolled in both a defined benefit and a defined contribution plan, implying that only about 37% of all pension-covered workers were enrolled in a defined benefit plan, usually in combination with a defined contribution plan. Thus, traditional pensions were provided to only a little more than a third of the workers enrolled in company plans.

The standard pension available to covered workers in the private sector is now a defined contribution pension rather than a defined benefit pension. In contrast, employees of the federal government and state and local governments continue to receive pension coverage under traditional plans. Not only are pension coverage rates much higher among public employees compared with private employees, the trend toward defined contribution coverage has been much more muted in the public sector. About 80% of pension-covered public employees are enrolled solely in a defined benefit plan, and only 14% are enrolled solely in a defined contribution plan.[3] More than five out of every six employees work in the private sector, however, so the decline in defined benefit pension plans outside of government employment has dramatically reduced the percentage of wage and salary workers covered by a traditional plan.

The decline of defined benefit pensions is viewed with alarm by many observers. Jacob Hacker sees the trend as part of a great "risk shift" that has transferred the burden of dealing with economic insecurity from employers to workers and their families.[4] Teresa Ghilarducci and other experts on the U.S. pension system worry that the shift to defined contribution pensions and particularly to voluntary 401(k) pensions will drastically reduce the retirement income security of American workers.[5]

While defined benefit pensions have many advantages, especially for workers who are employed for many years in the same firm, they have serious shortcomings from the point of view of people who work intermittently or who work for many employers over the course of a career. Even workers who are lucky enough to enjoy lengthy careers with a single company can experience large losses in their defined benefit pensions if their employer goes bankrupt before they reach the normal retirement age in the pension plan.

For most young workers who are employed outside the public sector, the relative risks of defined benefit and defined contribution pensions are not easy to evaluate. Workers enrolled in a defined benefit plan do not have to worry about how pension funds are invested, nor do they face the burden of setting aside part of their wages in a retirement savings account. On the other hand, workers enrolled in a defined benefit pension do have to be concerned about whether their careers with an employer will last long enough for their pension credits to produce a good pension. If a company bankruptcy or a permanent layoff ends a worker's career with a company long before retirement age, the defined benefit pension promise may have little practical value. Private sector workers cannot reliably predict how long they will be employed by a given employer. For that reason, workers with little job tenure find it difficult to know whether they are better off in a defined benefit or a defined contribution plan. For most workers, the main advantage of a defined benefit pension is that they automatically accumulate pension credits under the plan, even if they lack the discipline to save and regardless of their investment knowledge. The main disadvantage of a defined benefit plan is that the value of the pension credits depends crucially on how long the worker is employed by the pension-sponsoring firm. If the worker's career with a firm is brief, the credits may be worthless. Whether the trend toward defined contribution plans and away from defined benefit pensions is bad news for a particular worker depends on facts that are known to a worker who is 55 but that are largely unknown to a worker who is 30.

THE VALUE OF PENSIONS AND PENSION PROMISES

Employer-sponsored pensions are an important source of old-age income, but they are not the biggest source of income for most of America's elderly. The single most important source of income for most retirees is a monthly Social Security check. As noted above, nearly all Americans who are 65 or older receive a Social Security pension, and Social Security payments account for a large fraction of their total income. A sizeable fraction of the aged receive a pension or annuity from an employer-sponsored retirement plan, though the exact percentage is uncertain. Estimates by the Employee Benefit Research Institute (EBRI) suggest that 35% of Americans who are 65 or older receive income from pensions or annuities other than Social Security. In 2006 these pensions provided almost one-fifth of the money income received by the aged. The Social Security Administration estimates that 41% of aged families receive retirement benefits other than those provided by Social Security and concurs that these benefits provide about one-fifth of the money income of aged families.[6] Both sets of estimates imply that employer pensions are received by at least one-third of America's elderly and account for roughly half the fraction of income that is provided by Social Security.

These estimates almost certainly understate the importance of employer-sponsored pensions. For one thing, about one American in seven who is 65 or older is still employed and has not yet fully retired. Wage income and self-employment earnings account for a sizeable share of the household income received by aged Americans who still work. When the working elderly retire completely, employer pensions will represent a bigger percentage of their incomes. Equally important, many workers who leave a job do not leave their retirement savings in their employer's pension plan. They withdraw their savings from the plan, and many invest their withdrawals in another retirement savings plan, such as an IRA. Much of the income received by aged households that is classified as "asset income" may thus be derived from savings originally accumulated in a company pension plan.

Retirement income from employer pensions will probably represent a bigger percentage of the incomes of future retirees. Social Security benefits are scheduled to decline as the normal retirement age is raised from 65 to 67. Benefits are likely to be reduced still further when Congress deals with the long-run funding problems of Social Security, which is now expected to have too little money to pay for scheduled benefits starting in 2041. Since future Social Security benefits will be shrinking as a percentage of workers' earnings, it is important to ensure that employer pensions are strengthened so they can make up part of the loss. The sharp decline in defined benefit pensions in the private sector raises two questions. Will this trend reduce employer pensions for future retirees? And if so, how can private pensions be reformed so they provide better income security for workers who retire in the next few decades?

INCOME SECURITY UNDER A DEFINED BENEFIT PENSION

There is abundant evidence that both workers and voters have a preference for traditional pensions. The Social Security program, which is broadly popular among both working and retired voters, offers defined benefit pensions. Unionized workers, who have a powerful voice in determining the compensation package offered by their employers, are much more likely to be covered by a defined benefit plan rather than a defined contribution plan. Nonunionized workers, who have less influence over the terms and conditions of their employment, are mostly covered by defined contribution pensions.[7]

Workers' partiality toward defined benefit pensions is understandable. A defined benefit plan promises a pension that replaces a predictable percentage of workers' final pay. In a defined benefit plan, specialists are responsible for managing pension fund reserves, and fund managers are usually more competent than workers to choose among investment alternatives. Because defined benefit pensions are ordinarily paid out as lifetime annuities, retirees do not need to manage their own retirement nest eggs nor do they need to worry about depleting their retirement savings before they die. Since the mid 1970s, private sector defined benefit pensions have been insured by a government-backed corporation, the Pension Benefit Guaranty Corporation (PBGC). Workers who participate in a plan that is insured by PBGC are guaranteed minimum pension payments, even if the company sponsoring their plan goes bankrupt and pension fund reserves are too small to pay for promised benefits.[8] There is no equivalent government-provided insurance for defined contribution pensions.

The risks of defined benefit pensions are less obvious to many workers. To understand the risks associated with traditional pensions, it is necessary to understand how they are calculated and how the timing and duration of a career can affect the pension's value. Suppose that a worker is enrolled in a traditional plan that credits the worker with 1% of final salary for each year of participation in the plan. A worker with thirty years of service would thus be entitled to a pension of 30% (thirty times 1%) of the average wage at the end of a company career. Defined benefit plans have minimum vesting requirements before a worker becomes eligible for a pension, and most have both age and years of service requirements in determining the first age when a worker will be able to claim a pension. Suppose workers must be employed and covered by the plan for five years before becoming entitled to a pension. In addition, suppose workers who have accumulated at least twenty years of creditable service can claim a pension as early as age 55, while workers with between five and 19.99 years of service must wait until they are 62 before claiming a pension.

A standard way to measure pension generosity is to calculate the ratio of the pension to the worker's final wage. It is straightforward to determine the replacement rate offered by the defined benefit pension just described, assuming we measure the replacement rate using the final wage earned by the worker in her pension-covered job. Suppose the worker starts employment on her 20th birthday. The top chart in figure 2.2 shows how her replacement rate depends on the age at which she leaves this pension-covered job. If she quits at age 40 after working for twenty years, her pension will replace 20% (1% times twenty years) of her final wage on the job (see the top line in the figure). Note, however, that under the pension rules described in the previous paragraph, she will not be able to claim her first pension until she reaches age 55. By that age her wage, assuming she works for a new employer, is likely to be much higher than it was fifteen years earlier, when she was 40. If we measure the value of her pension in relation to the wage she could earn at the end of her career, say around age 62, her pension replacement rate looks smaller still. The lower broken line in the top panel of figure 2.2 shows the worker's replacement rate when we measure it using her final career wage (at age 62) instead of her final wage as a pension-covered employee. If the worker quits her pension-covered job at age 40, the replacement rate under this definition is only 8% rather than 20%. If she quits her job at 50, the replacement rate is 21.5% instead of 30%. Of course, if the worker leaves her pension-covered job at age 62, the replacement rate under both definitions is the same—42%.

The replacement rate under defined benefit plans usually looks lower when we use a worker's end-of-career wage instead of her end-of-job wage to estimate the amount of earnings replaced by the pension. The wages that workers earn over their careers generally rise as workers grow older, at least through age 50 or 55 when earnings tend to level off. The lower panel of figure 2.2 shows the pattern of lifetime earnings among workers interviewed by the U.S. Census Bureau, adjusted to reflect the fact that economy-wide real wages and consumer prices both rise as a worker gets older.[9] The top line in the chart shows the worker's annual wage at successive ages when wages are measured in contemporaneous prices. The lower line shows annual wages measured in constant prices (that is, in terms of consumer prices prevailing when the worker was 20). The faster the growth of wages over time, the bigger the discrepancy between the replacement rates estimated under the two definitions.

The top panel in figure 2.2 provides a rough indication of the financial risk workers face as a result of uncertainty about how long their

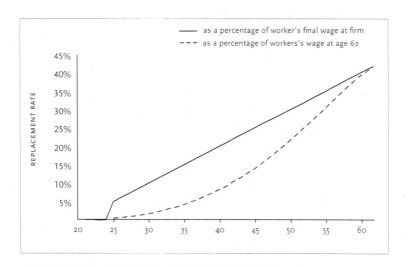

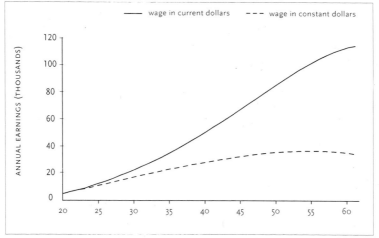

Figure 2.2   Replacement rate under defined benefit pension for worker who starts job at age 20 and leaves job at the indicated age   [Source: Author's calculations.]

pension-covered jobs will last. When employed for a full career by a company that offers traditional pensions, a worker's ultimate pension will replace a predictable percentage of the worker's final career wage. But when a worker's career is interrupted by a quit or layoff, the ultimate

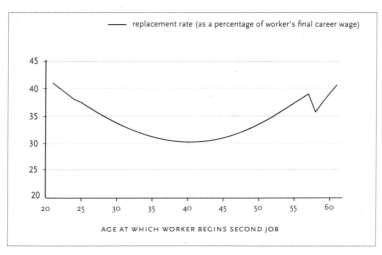

Figure 2.3   Pension replacement rate for worker who starts working at age 20 and holds two different jobs covered by a defined benefit pension   [Source: Author's calculations.]

replacement rate can fall far short of the replacement rate advertised in the pension plan formula. Under the rules of the pension we have been considering, a worker who begins her job at age 20 and is dismissed at age 45 is entitled to receive a pension that replaces 25% of her final pay. Yet this worker will ultimately receive a pension that replaces only 14% of her expected wage when she is near the end of her career. In calculating this replacement rate, I have assumed that the worker holds only one job covered by a traditional pension. After she loses this job, she works for employers who do not offer a pension. Suppose instead the laid-off worker finds another job that is covered by a pension. Let us also assume the defined benefit pension provided by the second job is calculated under the same rules and benefit formula we have discussed so far. Under these assumptions, the worker is employed for a full career in jobs that offer identical defined benefit pensions. Figure 2.3 shows the relationship between the age of the worker's layoff from her first job and the replacement rate she will obtain, measured as a percentage of the worker's expected wage when she is 62. (The worker is assumed to work every year from age 20 to age 62.) Although the pension formula promises a replacement rate of 42% based on the worker's forty-two years of covered employment, her actual replacement rate will fall short of this target, no matter what her age when she is laid off from her first job. If the layoff occurs at age 21, she will not qualify for a pension from her first job, and the pension from her second job will be based on only forty-one years of service. If the layoff occurs when she is 40, after twenty years of service on her first job, she will receive a replacement rate of 8% for her first job and 22% for her second job. This yields a combined replacement rate of 30%, more than one-quarter below the replacement rate implied by the defined benefit pension formula. If inflation is higher than the 3% rate I have assumed in these calculations, the combined replacement rate will be even lower than 30%. Few workers hold only one or two jobs over their careers, as assumed in the examples so far. As the number of lifetime jobs increases, the replacement rate provided by traditional plans tends to decline.

The lesson of these calculations is simple. Even though defined benefit pensions offer many advantages, their actual value to a particular worker depends crucially on the timing and duration of the worker's years of covered employment under a plan. If the worker's covered employment is interrupted as a result of a quit or layoff, the ultimate value of the pension can be low in relation to the worker's earnings when she is near retirement. The replacement rate implied by the defined benefit formula will then give a very misleading indicator of the replacement rate a worker is likely to receive.

COMPARING DEFINED BENEFIT AND DEFINED CONTRIBUTION PENSIONS

The easiest way to measure the generosity of a defined benefit pension is to determine the replacement rate it provides to new retirees. In contrast, the easiest way to measure the generosity of a defined contribution pension is to measure the annual amount that employers promise to contribute to the plan. In most cases, the contribution to defined contribution plans is expressed as a percentage of the worker's pay. Obviously, a 10% employer contribution is more generous than a 5% contribution. In many defined contribution plans, including nearly all 401(k) plans, the total contribution amount represents a joint decision of the employer and the worker. The employer may make a fixed percentage contribution and allow the employee to make voluntary contributions on top of that. Alternatively, the employer might match the employee's voluntary contribution up to some maximum amount, such as 3% of wages, and then allow workers to make additional voluntary but unmatched contributions.

One way to express the generosity of the employer's defined contribution plan is to calculate the average contribution the employer makes to workers' defined contribution accounts, measured as a percentage of the company's payroll. However, this ignores the fact that workers may be able to make voluntary contributions on top of those made by the employer. Workers can obtain sizeable tax advantages for voluntary contributions. Contributions to a 401(k) plan are not subject to income taxes in the year in which they are made, and the investment earnings on pension account balances are not taxed until they are withdrawn from the account. Critics of the trend toward 401(k)-type retirement plans point out that some eligible workers do not elect to participate in the plans offered to them. Many workers make voluntary contributions that are too low to provide adequate incomes in retirement. In 2004 about one-fifth of workers who were eligible to enroll in 401(k) plans failed to do so. Among eligible workers under age 30, about four out of every ten eligible workers failed to enroll in a 401(k) plan. Only a small percentage of workers who elect to participate in 401(k) plans make the maximum possible contribution to the plan, and many make contributions that are small in relation to the contribution needed to assure a comfortable retirement.[10]

A crucial feature of most current defined contribution plans is the decision-making responsibility placed on the shoulders of workers. In many plans, workers must elect to participate in the plan, and in most plans, workers must decide on the total amount of contribution that will be made. Even though workers' contributions are tax favored and may be generously subsidized by an employer match, workers must decide for themselves the total contribution that will be made. In theory, workers will make rational, farsighted decisions based on their assessment of the relative importance of current versus deferred compensation. In contrast to typical defined benefit plans, most 401(k) plans allow workers to decide for themselves how to divide their compensation between current money wages and future retirement benefits. Many critics of the trend toward defined contribution plans are skeptical that workers are equipped to make this kind of decision in a farsighted way and fear that, as a result, worker contributions to voluntary retirement plans will fall short of what is needed to replace a large fraction of their wages.

Can we say whether a particular defined benefit pension is more or less generous than a defined contribution pension? The simplest way to make this determination is to calculate the contributions needed to pay for the two kinds of pensions. The pension requiring the larger contribution is the one that is more generous. The calculation is straightforward in the case of a defined contribution pension because the contribution is usually expressed as a percentage of the worker's pay. In the case of a defined benefit pension, the calculation is more complicated because we can only calculate the employer's required contribution after determining the size of the monthly pension and the age at which the worker's pension will begin. These are only known once a worker has completed her career or been laid off from her pension-covered job. With this information in hand, however, we can calculate the annual contribution the employer must make in order to fund the defined benefit pension it has promised to the departing worker.

Figure 2.4 shows the results of these calculations for selected workers who begin and end their employment at a variety of ages.[11] The required contribution for each worker is calculated as a percentage of the total wages the worker earns up through the point she retires, quits, or is laid off. The top line in figure 2.4 shows required contributions for workers who begin their job at age 20. Successive points along that line show the required defined benefit pension contributions for workers who leave their job at successively higher ages. For example, a worker who leaves her job at age 21 will not require any pension contribution because she works too few years to qualify for a pension. A worker who leaves her job upon attaining age 25, after five years of covered employment, will qualify for a pension, and the employer will have to contribute 2.4% of the worker's wages to pay for the pension. As the worker's years of service with the company increase, the company's required contributions to pay for the pension will also rise.

Whether the defined benefit pension is more or less generous than a defined contribution pension depends on the defined contribution plan's annual contribution rate and the worker's years of service under the plan. For example, a defined contribution plan with a 6% annual contribution rate is more generous than the traditional plan for workers

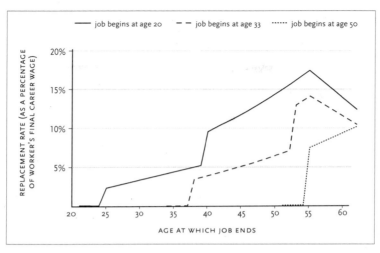

Figure 2.4   Required defined benefit pension contribution for workers who begin and end their jobs at selected ages   [Source: Author's calculations.]

whose employment ends before age 40. At every job-leaving age from 21 through 39, the required contribution rate to fund the traditional pension is less than 6%. On the other hand, the 6% defined contribution plan is substantially less generous than the defined benefit plan in the case of workers who are employed twenty years or longer in the firm. The lesson is plain. Workers who expect relatively short job tenures should prefer to work in firms offering defined contribution pensions; workers who anticipate long job tenures should prefer coverage under a traditional plan.

Figure 2.4 also gives results for workers who begin their employment at later ages. The middle line shows required pension contributions for workers who begin jobs at age 33; the line to the right shows required contributions for those starting work at age 50. If the worker leaves the firm during the first five years after a job begins, the required contribution is zero because the worker will have too little employment to become eligible for a pension. After exactly five years of employment, there is an immediate jump in the required contribution for the worker's pension. Note that the jump is bigger for workers who start their jobs at later ages. Even though all workers are eligible for a 5% replacement-rate pension after their fifth year on the job, the number of years they must wait before their pension begins is shorter in the case of workers who begin their jobs at a later age. The 25-year-old who is entitled to a 5% replacement-rate pension must wait thirty-seven years for her first pension payment, whereas the 55-year-old will receive her first pension in just seven years. A longer time period between job exit and benefit claiming allows the insurance company to earn investment income on its investments for a greater number of years. Investment income can thus pay for a larger percentage of the future cost of the pension. The employer's contribution can therefore be smaller in the case of workers who begin and end their covered employment when they are comparatively young.[12] The lesson from this comparison is that the payoff from coverage under a traditional plan can be considerably greater for older employees compared with younger employees, even if the two workers expect to have the same tenure with the firm.

In a purely financial sense, there is no way to predict under all circumstances whether workers ought to favor defined benefit over defined contribution pensions. Depending on the worker's age and expected tenure with a firm, she may rationally favor either kind of pension. Older workers and workers who anticipate a lengthy job tenure with the same firm might rationally prefer to be covered under a traditional plan. Younger workers and workers who believe that a long job tenure is unlikely should prefer defined contribution pensions. One advantage of traditional pensions for all classes of workers is that the financial risk of poor investment returns is borne by the employer. This advantage can appear quite attractive when stock and bond prices are falling sharply, as has occurred many times over the past century. However, workers who anticipate holding jobs with many employers might think that this advantage of defined benefit pensions is more than offset by the portability of defined contribution savings. A worker who holds fifteen lifetime jobs, each covered by a defined contribution plan, will usually accumulate more retirement savings than a worker who holds fifteen lifetime jobs, each covered by a traditional plan. And this is true even if stock and bond prices fall sharply around the time a worker plans to retire.

The estimates in figure 2.4 show that defined benefit pension accumulations are heavily "back loaded." That is, workers must be employed for a substantial amount of time before they begin to accumulate pension rights that are expensive for their employers to provide. One reason that employers might find this arrangement attractive is that it provides strong incentives for employees to remain with the firm. If workers can be induced to stay with the firm, the company might find it much easier to recoup its investments in worker training. Note, however, that the traditional plan also provides incentives for long-service workers to leave the firm when they attain the earliest pension-claiming age. In the defined benefit plan illustrated in figure 2.4, long-tenure workers may be induced to leave the firm at age 55, the earliest benefit-claiming age for workers who have accumulated at least twenty years of service. Long-service workers who remain on the payroll after age 55 can experience a decline in compensation with the fall of the required employer pension contribution. Thus, in addition to providing workers with retirement incomes, traditional pensions may be an instrument to encourage young and middle-aged workers to remain with the firm longer and to encourage faster job exit among older workers. Defined contribution pensions could be structured to achieve the same goals, but they seldom are. Most defined contribution plans provide employer contributions that represent a fixed percentage of pay, regardless of the worker's age or years of service.

THE DECLINE IN JOB TENURE

One factor affecting the relative attractiveness of defined benefit versus defined contribution pensions is the decline in job tenure of employees who are nearing the end of their careers. As we have seen, traditional pensions are more attractive when workers can be reasonably certain they will work long enough with an employer to accumulate pension credits that will translate into a good pension. However, job tenures have declined since the early 1980s for typical middle-aged workers. The U.S. Bureau of Labor Statistics has obtained consistent survey information about workers' job tenure since 1983 (see figure 2.5). In the years since then, job tenure for men has fallen at all ages past 35 while the median tenure of women workers has risen modestly except in the oldest age category where it has also declined.

Given the upward trend in women's employment rates, it is not surprising that men's and women's job tenure patterns looked more

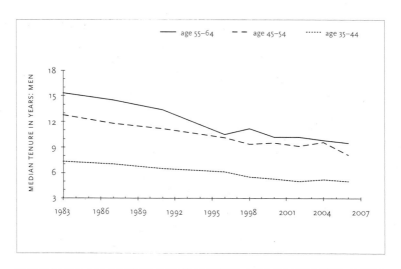

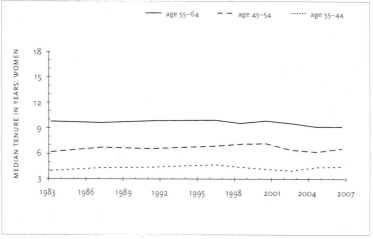

Figure 2.5   Median years of job tenure with current employer among U.S. wage and salary workers, by age of worker, 1983–2006   [Sources: U.S. Bureau of Labor Statistics, "Employee Tenure in 2004," *News* (U.S. Department of Labor) 04-1829 (September 21, 2004), http://www.bls.gov/news.release/archives/tenure_09212004.pdf; and U.S. Bureau of Labor Statistics, "Employee Tenure in 2006," *News* (U.S. Department of Labor) 06-1563 (September 8, 2006), http://www.bls.gov/news.release/archives/tenure_09082006.pdf.]

similar in 2006 than they did in 1983. Women are nowadays more likely to remain steadily in the workforce than was the case before 1983. What is surprising is that men's and women's tenure patterns have converged mainly because average male tenure has *declined* rather than because female tenures have increased. Between 1983 and 2006, the median tenure of male wage earners between 45 and 54 years old fell 4.7 years (37%), and for those between 55 and 64 years old, it fell 5.8 years (38%). Workers' average tenure in jobs depends on their willingness to remain in the job as well as employers' job separation policies. If workers' aspirations to hold on to their jobs are just as strong today as they were in 1983, the decline in average job tenure reflects an increased willingness or need on the part of employers to discharge their workers before they accumulate long tenure on the job. Many observers believe that modern companies show less loyalty to their line employees and are more likely to dismiss them to obtain better financial results, even when the company is profitable and faces no immediate risk of bankruptcy. Whatever the reason for the trend, the evidence in figure 2.5 shows that permanent job separation is now more common for medium- and long-tenure workers than it was in the early 1980s. If workers are less likely to reach their middle or late fifties in a long-tenure job, a defined benefit pension can look a lot less attractive than a defined contribution pension.

Analysts at Boston College's Center for Retirement Research point out that the drop in average job tenure at older ages may be a byproduct of the decline in traditional pensions.[13] As private employers have adopted defined contribution plans, such as 401(k)s, in preference to traditional plans, they have reduced back-loading in their compensation plans, reducing the incentive for employees to accumulate long tenure on their jobs. Most workers with a defined contribution pension face no loss in the value of their pension savings if they quit their jobs and find work with another employer. In contrast, an employee covered by a traditional plan can miss out on a big boost in her pension if she quits her job early. As illustrated in figure 2.4, workers hired in their twenties or early thirties can enjoy a big gain in defined benefit pension benefits if they manage to accumulate at least twenty years on the job. Although the details will differ from one plan to another, this pattern is common to nearly all defined benefit plans. As traditional plans have been phased out or scaled back in older companies and as defined contribution plans have been adopted by younger companies, the payoff to accumulating long job tenures has been reduced, almost certainly contributing to the job tenure trends shown in figure 2.5. It should be noted, however, that many young companies have introduced or adopted new components of the pay package, such as nonmarketable employee stock options, which tend to bind workers to their employers. Although stock options have a different structure than defined benefit pensions, they may provide equally powerful incentives to keep workers attached to the firm.

Even if it is true that the decline in traditional pensions has contributed to the drop in average job tenure, many young workers seem to be aware that they are now less likely to reach their middle fifties employed by the same firm that employed them when they were in their twenties or thirties. Under these circumstances, it is rational for them to discount the value of a defined benefit pension promise and prefer the portable benefits promised under a defined contribution plan.

PENSIONS AND WORKER PSYCHOLOGY

Much of the discussion so far rests on the assumption that workers' thinking about pension plans is dominated by hardheaded calculations about the financial advantages and disadvantages of different kinds of retirement plans. Under this assumption, popular with professors of economics and finance, workers tend to choose employers and compensation plans based on farsighted and deliberate assessments of the potential risks and rewards of different pension arrangements. This assumption may be correct for some workers but is unlikely to be true for the majority of them. Many observers, including a few economists, are skeptical that workers think about pensions in the farsighted and logical way just described. One reason that the government offers Social Security, that companies provide pensions, and that unions agitate for bigger pensions is lack of confidence that workers will make sensible provision for old age on their own. The basic rationale for employer and government pensions is that it is better to organize retirement saving collectively rather than to rely on the unaided efforts of individual workers.

A traditional defined benefit pension helps solve three problems that most workers face as they prepare for retirement. First, the plan automatically sets aside a portion of current compensation for savings in a retirement account. Money in that account only becomes available when the worker is old or retired. Workers do not have to rely on their own judgment to select a retirement saving rate, nor do they have to rely on self-discipline to stick with the saving plan they adopt. Second, the money set aside in the retirement plan is managed by specialists who are knowledgeable about investing. Workers are not asked to rely on their own investment expertise, which may be limited. Third, when workers reach the end of their careers, their retirement nest eggs are converted into monthly annuity payments that last for the remainder of their lives. Workers do not need to worry about living so long or spending their nest egg so fast that they exhaust their retirement savings before they die.

A mandatory defined contribution pension can also solve these three problems, but many mandatory plans solve only one or two of them. A voluntary defined contribution pension, such as the ones offered under most 401(k) plans, may not solve any of the three problems just mentioned. In most 401(k) plans, it is left to workers to decide how much, if anything, to contribute to the plan. Under voluntary plans, workers can and do elect to save too little. Workers are asked to decide for themselves how to invest their retirement savings, usually from a menu of investment options selected by their employer. Many workers are not competent to make investment decisions, and the poor performance of their investments reflects this fact. When employment under a defined contribution plan ends, a worker may not be offered the option to buy a life annuity. If a retirement nest egg is kept in an ordinary investment account rather than converted into an annuity, the retiree faces the risk of outliving his or her savings.

Companies that rely on workers to make their own decisions about retirement saving and investment have made a reasonable choice if workers make these decisions competently. The same choice looks riskier when a large fraction of workers base saving and investment decisions on incomplete or incorrect information, short time horizons, and bad reasoning. Voluntary defined contribution pensions require workers to assume more responsibility to save for retirement, to allocate their pension savings across different investment options, and to plan the timing of asset withdrawal during retirement. When companies adopt a worker-directed defined contribution plan, they should be confident that most workers will make prudent decisions. Serious planning errors, either when the worker is employed or when he is retired, can lead to serious hardship if the worker's error is a big one. By the time a retired worker discovers he has saved too little or has invested unwisely, he may have little opportunity to undo his mistake by increasing his saving rate or going back to work.

Whether declining enrollment in traditional pensions poses a major risk hinges on the planning abilities and investment acumen of American workers. If workers do not save enough or if they are not competent to invest their retirement savings, the trend toward voluntary defined contribution pensions represents a threat to retirement income security. On the other hand, if the great majority of workers can devise and follow through on a sensible saving plan, the movement toward voluntary defined contribution plans does not represent much of a problem.

Observers disagree on whether workers do a good or bad job of saving for retirement. When polled about their preparations for retirement, large minorities of American workers say they have given no thought to the subject, have set aside little in pension and other savings accounts, and lack confidence they will be able to afford retirement. In fact, many workers reach old age with very little savings. Annamaria Lusardi analyzed the 1992 wealth holdings of workers who were between 50 and 61 years old, before any of them had retired.[14] Most of the workers were within a decade of retirement. Those in the bottom one-tenth of the wealth distribution had no wealth at all except the promise of a Social Security check. Even workers at the twenty-fifth percentile had very little wealth. At that point in the distribution, workers' total wealth holdings, including equity in a home or business, defined contribution pension accumulations, and vehicles, amounted to about $41,000 (in 2007 dollars). If all this wealth were sold and converted into a lifetime annuity, it would provide workers with an income of less than $300 a month. One-quarter of 50–61-year-old workers in Lusardi's sample had even less wealth. Lusardi is not alone in finding low pension accumulations and wealth holdings among workers nearing retirement. A number of economists and financial planners have published studies showing that middle-aged and older U.S. workers face large savings shortfalls compared with the nest eggs they would need to retire at the standard retirement age.[15]

On the other hand, it is not obvious that a large percentage of workers have a nest egg that is substantially below what is needed to maintain adequate consumption in retirement, where "adequate" is interpreted to mean that workers' consumption in retirement represents a very high percentage of the real consumption they enjoyed before they retired.[16] Retirees who have little wealth or income can rely on Social Security and public assistance to support a minimal level of old-age consumption. While many retired workers live on very low incomes, most of these same workers had low incomes when they were employed. There is little evidence in either the income or poverty statistics to suggest that Americans who retired in the recent past have a noticeably lower standard of living than the working-age population.[17] There is thus little direct evidence that clearly shows retirees saved too little when they were active workers. Of course, the good fortune of some retirees is due to their good luck in being covered by a traditional pension plan. This does not account for the situation of older Americans who have moderate or below-average incomes, because comparatively few of them derive much of their income from private defined benefit pensions.[18]

The main reason that middle-class and low-income aged households fare rather well compared with middle-class and low-income workers is that they currently receive generous replacement rates under Social Security. Even if they did not save much on their own, the availability of decent Social Security and public assistance benefits prevents most of them from falling into poverty. If future Social Security benefits are scaled back to make public pensions more affordable, it is less clear whether workers who do not save will enjoy such a comfortable retirement.

Workers' investment skills are open to question. Analysts who have surveyed workers about their financial knowledge usually come away disappointed. Annamaria Lusardi and Olivia Mitchell found that "...half the respondents...in our [survey] cannot make a simple calculation regarding interest rates over a five-year period and do not know the difference between nominal and real interest rates. An even larger percentage of respondents do not know that holding a single company stock is riskier than holding a stock mutual fund."[19] The investment behavior of participants in worker-directed defined contribution plans offers grounds for concern. Many participants fail to diversify their asset holdings, allocate too much of their portfolio to their own company's stock, allocate too little to equity, neglect to periodically re-balance their portfolios to maintain a consistent asset allocation, and are excessively influenced in choosing assets by the specific range and ordering of investment options in their retirement plan. Workers who invest mainly or solely in very safe assets, such as a money market fund, need a very high saving rate to achieve a good pension replacement rate. On the other hand, workers who invest heavily in their own company's stock expose themselves to excessive risk. If their company should fail, they will lose not only their jobs but a large percentage of their retirement savings.

In spite of the shortcomings of individual investors, the aggregate performance of asset holdings in worker-directed 401(k) plans is only moderately worse than the performance of assets held in traditional defined benefit plans. There is some evidence, however, that assets held in IRAs obtain substantially worse returns than investments held in defined benefit pension funds.[20] A large percentage of pension savings that are originally accumulated in worker-directed defined contribution accounts will eventually be transferred into IRAs, where they will be invested with fewer constraints than the ones imposed in 401(k) plans.

REFORMING THE SYSTEM

Given its long-term financial problems, Social Security will almost certainly provide less generous benefits in the future than it provides to today's retirees. One reason is that the normal retirement age in Social Security is rising gradually, increasing from 65 to 67. Unless workers postpone the age at which they begin to collect pensions by two full years, the increase in the retirement age has the effect of reducing the value of Social Security benefits relative to workers' pre-retirement wages. Another reason monthly benefits will fall is that Medicare premiums are deducted from benefit checks, and Medicare premiums are expected to rise substantially. In view of the expected pressure on future Social Security payments, it seems sensible to strengthen the private retirement system.

Over the past three decades, Congress has changed the law to make it easier for companies to offer simple defined contribution pensions to their workers, notably through 401(k) plans and Simplified Employee Pension IRAs (SEP-IRA plans). Many companies have taken advantage of these reforms by establishing voluntary, worker-directed defined contribution pension plans for their employees. At the same time, many employers with traditional retirement plans have scrapped or scaled back their defined benefit pensions. New companies are much less likely to establish traditional defined benefit plans for their employees. The private retirement system now covers approximately the same percentage of the workforce as it did in the late 1970s, but the percentage of pension-covered workers who are offered traditional pensions has fallen dramatically. The new employer-based retirement system emphasizes employee decision making, both in the determination of annual pension contributions and in the allocation of contributions across different kinds of investments.

For farsighted and well-informed workers, the new system offers some notable advantages. Employer contributions under the new system are easily portable from one job to the next. Workers who experience or anticipate relatively short job tenures can accumulate more retirement savings under modern defined contribution plans than would have been possible under traditional plans. The new system has important drawbacks, however. Even workers who have the self-discipline to save are exposed to the risk that their retirement nest eggs will be smaller than planned because asset prices fall just before they retire. The risks are even more severe for workers who lack the self-control to set aside a fixed percentage of their pay in a retirement account. Because worker-directed defined contribution plans require workers to choose their retirement investments, employees who are not financially literate can find themselves at risk of accumulating very small pensions.

Many critics of worker-directed defined contribution plans think it would be a good idea to bring traditional defined benefit pensions back into the workplace. This may be true in the case of workers who expect to enjoy long careers with the same employer, but it is less obviously true for the very large proportion of the workforce that will never experience a long career with a single employer. In addition, it is unrealistic to think there will be a resurgence of traditional pensions anytime soon. For most private employers, the administrative and regulatory burden of establishing and maintaining a defined benefit plan is high relative to that of maintaining a defined contribution plan. The high administrative burden of defined benefit plans makes many employers reluctant to adopt them.[21] Congress is unlikely to reduce the regulatory burden on defined benefit plans, because the plans are covered by government-provided insurance. This insurance is financed by premium payers, who have a stake in requiring defined benefit plans to comply with strict regulations on pension funding. It is more realistic to consider reforms that would mitigate the shortcomings of worker-directed defined contribution plans. Congress and President George W. Bush have already taken steps in this direction, but additional steps are needed.

One desirable change would be to introduce more sensible "default options" into existing defined contribution plans. In most plans, workers must make two crucial decisions if they want to establish and pursue a good retirement saving plan. The first is the choice of a monthly contribution amount. The second is the allocation of the employer and worker contributions into different investment options. In most current defined contribution plans, the default options do not produce desirable outcomes.[22] Many newly hired workers must positively elect to participate in a defined contribution plan by specifying a desired contribution amount. Contributions are then taken out of the worker's pretax wages, and they may be matched (up to a limit) by contributions from the employer. An alternative default option is to withhold automatically the maximum amount of employee wages that are eligible for the employer match. Another default option might be a minimum contribution amount, say 6% of wages, under the assumption that a 6% contribution is needed to accumulate a minimally adequate pension. In whatever way the default option is determined, it should establish a contribution pattern that will result in meaningful pensions for typical workers. Workers can still elect to reduce their contributions to zero, but this option should never represent the default. Experience suggests that many more workers will make a positive retirement contribution if the default option specifies a positive contribution rather than a zero contribution.

Both voluntary and mandatory defined contribution pension plans usually require workers to specify the assets in which their contributions will be invested. In many plans, the default investment option is the safest asset included on the menu of alternatives offered by the plan. For example, a standard default option might be a money market fund or a very low-risk bond fund. Neither kind of asset is an appropriate choice for a young or middle-aged worker. An alternative default option would be a mutual fund that has been selected by financial specialists to represent a good mix of assets for retirement saving. Many mutual fund companies now offer life-cycle funds. This kind of fund contains a mix of stocks, bonds, and safe assets tailored to reflect the investor's age. As investors grow older, the investment portfolio is gradually changed to include a less risky mix of assets, reflecting the fact that workers near retirement usually have less tolerance for risk. Changes in federal law and regulation over the past couple of years have made it easier for employers to select riskier default investment options in their 401(k) plans. A worthwhile reform would be to require firms to provide an investment default option that combines a mix of stocks and bonds that is thought to be prudent given the worker's age.

Most critics of the private sector pension system doubt whether these reforms go far enough. I agree. However, the main problem with the current system is not the increased emphasis on worker-directed defined contribution pensions. Rather, the main problem is that about half of private sector workers are not offered the option of participating in an employer-based retirement plan. Nearly everyone finds it easier to save for retirement when savings are automatically withheld from a paycheck. If the money is deposited in a retirement account before it is received by workers, workers are more likely to end each year with some extra resources with which to finance their retirement.

One needed reform is to require private employers that do not currently offer pensions to establish voluntary SEP-IRA plans for their employees. The new law does not need to oblige employers to make contributions to these plans, but employers should be required to manage payroll withholding for retirement accounts on behalf of their employees. The actual management of workers' retirement investments could be the responsibility of a qualified financial institution selected by the employer, such as a mutual fund company.

Of course, this new mandate would impose additional administrative burdens on employers that do not currently offer retirement plans. Because of the extra administrative expense, many small businesses and larger companies that employ temporary or intermittent workers will fiercely oppose the reform. For that reason, employers should be offered another option for managing the payroll savings contributions of their employees. The federal government should create a new public entity that collects the payroll contributions of workers employed by companies that do not offer retirement plans. The new public entity would be charged with the responsibility for managing a universal SEP-IRA plan covering all employees who are not currently offered a pension by their employer. The plan should offer a menu of ten to twelve investment alternatives as well as a default investment option that combines several basic asset types into a single age-appropriate investment portfolio. The public entity that serves as trustee of the universal SEP-IRA plan would select fund managers for each basic fund from among qualified financial institutions. Fund managers would be selected on the basis of periodic competitions to ensure that fund management costs are kept as low as possible. The public trustee of the universal SEP-IRA would serve as record keeper and manager of individual workers' accounts. Employers would only be required to determine workers' choices with respect to contribution levels and initial investment allocations and to send periodic contributions to the public trustee on behalf of their workers. If payroll withholding for the universal SEP-IRA accounts were integrated with the current system of withholding for Social Security taxes, the administrative burden on employers would be small. After workers make an initial investment allocation through their employers, they would be free to change their allocation by notifying the public trustee of their new investment choices.

The main goal of a universal SEP-IRA system is to provide universal access to automatic payroll withholding for retirement saving. This goal should be accomplished while minimizing the administrative burden on employers required to offer workplace-based pensions. The public trustee of the universal SEP-IRA plan should be charged with holding down the administrative and funds management costs of the scheme, since these will ultimately be borne by workers. The current private retirement system falls far short of offering universal access to workplace-based pensions. Estimates by the Congressional Research Service show that only 53% of 25–64-year-old private sector employees were offered workplace pensions by their employers in 2006. Among part-time workers, only 38% were offered workplace pensions.[23] Except in the youngest age groups and lowest income groups, participation in voluntary 401(k)-type plans is high, which suggests that participation in the private retirement system would be considerably higher if all employers were required to offer a workplace retirement plan to their employees. Such a mandate would greatly improve the current workplace retirement system.

NOTES

Acknowledgment: The views are the author's alone and do not reflect those of the Brookings Institution.

1   Ken McDonnell, "Income of the Elderly Population Age 65 and Over, 2006," *EBRI Notes* (Employee Benefit Research Institute) 28, no. 12 (December 2007): 10–15.

2   Craig Copeland, "Employment-Based Retirement Plan Participation: Geographic Differences and Trends, 2006," *EBRI Issue Brief* (Employee Benefit Research Institute) 311 (November 2007): 7.

3   Six percent of pension-covered public employees are enrolled in both a defined benefit and a defined contribution plan. Alicia H. Munnell and Mauricio Soto, "State and Local Plans Are Different from Private Plans," *State and Local Pension Plans Brief* (Center for Retirement Research at Boston College) 1 (November 2007): 3.

4   Jacob S. Hacker, *The Great Risk Shift: the Assault on American Jobs, Families, Health Care, and Retirement and How You Can Fight Back* (Oxford: Oxford University Press, 2006).

5   Teresa Ghilarducci, "The End of Retirement," *Monthly Review* 58, no. 1 (May 2006).

6   McDonnell, "Income of the Elderly," 11; and U.S. Social Security Administration, *Income of the Aged Chartbook, 2004* (Washington, DC, 2006), 3 and 21. Note that the EBRI estimates refer to incomes received in 2006 while the Social Security Administration numbers refer to incomes received in 2004.

7   The AFL-CIO estimates that 67% of unionized workers participate in a defined benefit pension plan. The comparable defined benefit coverage rate among nonunionized workers is only 15%. Among workers who are covered by a pension plan, the percentage of unionized workers in a defined benefit plan is also much higher than it is among pension-covered nonunionized workers. AFL-CIO, "Union Workers have Better Health Care and Pensions," http://www.aflcio.org/joinaunion/why/uniondifference/uniondiff6.cfm (accessed April 24, 2008). See also Ghilarducci, "The End of Retirement."

8   See Employee Benefit Research Institute, "Basics of the Pension Benefit Guaranty Corporation (PBGC)," *Facts from EBRI* (January 2007).

9   U.S. Bureau of the Census, *Money Income in the United States: 1995*, series P60-193 (Washington, DC, 1996). Estimates I derived from the Census Bureau tabulations show the relationship between age and average wage in a single calendar year: 1995. The estimates shown in the bottom panel of figure 2.2 assume that economy-wide real wages increase 1.5% a year over the course of a worker's career and price inflation averages 3% a year.

10 Alicia H. Munnell and Annika Sundén, "401(k) Plans Are Still Coming Up Short," *Issue in Brief* (Center for Retirement Research at Boston College) 43 (March 2006): 3.

11 Once again I assume that the worker is enrolled in a defined benefit plan that credits the worker with 1% of her final salary for each year of participation in the plan, that the worker must be covered by the plan for five years before becoming entitled to a pension, that workers who have accumulated at least twenty years of service can claim a pension at age 55, and that workers with between five and 19.99 years of service must wait until age 62 before claiming a pension. In order to calculate the contribution the employer must make to fund the worker's pension, I assume that the worker's lifetime wages follow the pattern shown in the lower panel of figure 2.2, that the inflation rate is 3% a year, and that the interest rate is 4.5%. I have used life expectancy tables created by the Social Security Administration to determine the present value of the pension.

12 The shape of the wage profile over a worker's career also affects the cost of a defined benefit pension when it is measured relative to the worker's cumulative wages in covered employment. However, the dominant factor that makes it more costly to fund pensions for workers who begin their pension-covered jobs late in a career is that there are fewer years between the worker's job exit and her eligibility to receive a monthly pension.

13 Alicia H. Munnell, Kelly Haverstick, and Geoffrey Sanzenbacher, "Job Tenure and Pension Coverage," CRR WP 2006-18 (working paper, Center for Retirement Research at Boston College, October 2006).

14 Annamaria Lusardi, "Explaining Why So Many People Do Not Save," CRR WP 2001-5 (working paper, Center for Retirement Research at Boston College, September 2001).

15 B. Douglas Bernheim, "Is the Baby Boom Generation Preparing Adequately for Retirement?" (technical report, Merrill Lynch and Company, 1992); Bernheim, "The Merrill Lynch Baby Boom Retirement Index: Update '95" (Merrill Lynch and Company, 1995); and James F. Moore and Olivia S. Mitchell, "Projected Retirement Wealth and Saving Adequacy," in *Forecasting Retirement Needs and Retirement*

Wealth, ed. Olivia. S. Mitchell, Brett Hammond, and Anna M. Rappaport (Philadelphia: University of Pennsylvania Press, 2000).

16 John Karl Scholz, Ananth Seshadri, and Surachai Khitatrakun, "Are Americans Saving 'Optimally' for Retirement?" *Journal of Political Economy* 114, no. 4 (August 2006): 607–42.

17 Barry P. Bosworth, Gary Burtless, and Sarah E. Anders, "Capital Income Flows and the Relative Well-Being of America's Aged Population," CRR WP 2007-21 (working paper, Center for Retirement Research at Boston College, December 2007).

18 Only about 12% of elderly families in the bottom two-fifths of the elderly income distribution derive any income at all from private pensions or annuities, and the percentage of income received from this source is very small. Office of Policy, U.S. Social Security Administration, *Income of the Population 55 or Older, 2004* (Washington, DC, 2006), tables 1.6, 5.D2, and 6.A2.

19 Annamaria Lusardi and Olivia S. Mitchell, "Baby Boomer Retirement Security: The Roles of Planning, Financial Literacy, and Housing Wealth" NBER W12585 (working paper, National Bureau of Economic Research, October 2006).

20 Alicia H. Munnell, Mauricio Soto, Jerilyn Libby, and John Prinzivalli, "Investment Returns: Defined Benefit vs. 401(k) Plans," *Issue in Brief* (Center for Retirement Research at Boston College) 52 (September 2006).

21 The additional regulatory costs of defined benefit pensions compared with defined contribution pensions are documented by Robert L. Clark and Ann A. McDermed in *The Choice of Pension Plans in a Changing Regulatory Environment* (Washington, DC: AEI Press, 1990), chap. 7. In addition, employers introducing a new defined benefit plan are obliged to make premium contributions to the PBGC, whereas firms introducing a new defined contribution plan do not have to make such contributions.

22 For a good survey of the literature on the effects of changing pension plan default options, see John A. Turner, "Designing 401(k) Plans That Encourage Retirement Savings: Lessons From Behavioral Finance Research," *Issue Brief* (AARP Public Policy Institute) 80 (April 2006).

23 Patrick Purcell, "Pension Sponsorship and Participation: Summary of Recent Trends," *CRS Report* (Congressional Research Service) RL30122 (September 2007): 6.

CHAPTER THREE

Financial Market Turbulence and Social Security Reform

GARY BURTLESS

Social Security was created in the middle of the Great Depression. The dive in stock prices in 2008 and the drop in home values after 2006 offer painful reminders of why government-guaranteed pensions seemed like a good idea in the 1930s. President Franklin Roosevelt proposed the creation of Social Security back in 1935, a bit more than five years after the stock market crash of October 1929. The collapse of stock prices and the bankruptcy of thousands of farms, businesses, and banks wiped out the lifetime savings of millions of retirees and aging workers. Many industrial and trade union pension plans became insolvent, leaving former pensioners with no dependable source of income in old age. In view of the shakiness of private savings, it is not surprising that the President, Congress, and most American voters thought a public pension plan, backed by the taxing power of the federal government, was preferable to sole reliance on private retirement savings.

Today's Social Security program covers a much bigger fraction of the workforce and offers better income protection than the one established by President Roosevelt in the Great Depression. Like the original system, however, the current program provides workers with a reliable source of retirement income that is largely insulated from the risks of company bankruptcy and financial market turbulence. For Americans past age 65, Social Security now accounts for about 40% of total income. The share is even larger for elderly households with average and below-average incomes (see chapter Appendix).

The stock market turbulence in 2008 gives a vivid demonstration of the impact of falling asset prices on retirement incomes. Between October 31, 2007, and the close of trading on October 31, 2008, stock market prices in the United States fell 37.5%. Because consumer prices rose nearly 5% during the same period, newly retired workers who had invested all their savings in the American stock market saw the purchasing power of their nest eggs shrink more than 40%. In contrast, the inflation-adjusted value of Social Security benefits was essentially unaffected by the stock market slump.

Social Security pensions are not totally secure, of course. If Congress does not raise the contribution rate or trim benefits in the next three decades, the reserves of the system will be depleted shortly after 2040. At that point Social Security pensions will have to be cut or contributions into the system increased. If all the adjustment takes the form of a benefit cut, monthly pensions will have to be trimmed about 22% around the time the Social Security reserve fund is exhausted.[1]

Social Security's long-run funding problem is one reason critics of the program argue for full or partial privatization of the program. As recently as 2005, President George W. Bush urged Congress to adopt a reform plan that would have allowed workers to divert some of their Social Security contributions into private retirement accounts. The reform would have undermined Social Security funding over the next few decades because workers who opted into the new accounts would have sent smaller contributions to the existing system. Since Social Security's revenue base would be smaller, Congress would be forced to reduce monthly pensions or make large transfers from the Treasury to Social Security to assure that full benefits could be paid.

Individual account plans like the one proposed by President Bush differ from traditional Social Security in an important way. Each worker's private retirement benefit depends solely on the size of the worker's contributions and the success of the worker's investment strategy. Workers who make bigger contributions and earn better returns on their savings get larger pensions than workers who contribute less and earn lower returns. In contrast, workers' Social Security benefits depend on their average lifetime wages, their eligible dependents when they claim a pension, and the age at which a benefit is claimed. Workers who retire at the same age and with the same earnings records generally receive very similar benefits, regardless of the year in which they claim a pension or the ups and downs of asset prices.

A supposed advantage of individual retirement accounts is that they permit workers to earn a much better rate of return than they can obtain on their contributions to traditional Social Security. I have heard it claimed, for example, that workers will earn negative rates of return on their contributions to Social Security, while they can earn 7% or more on their contributions to a private retirement account. The comparison is incorrect and seriously misleading.[2] Most workers can expect to obtain positive real returns on their contributions to Social Security. Over the next few decades, only a few of them could obtain significantly higher returns if the system were partly or fully privatized.

INVESTMENT RISK

There is a more basic problem with individual retirement accounts, however, one that is highlighted by the recent market turmoil. It is hard to predict how much retirement income will be produced by a private savings plan. In this respect, President Bush's proposed individual accounts were very much like the private retirement saving options already available to U.S. workers. The value of the assets held in the account can go down as well as up, unless all the savings are held in very conservative government-issued securities. Of course, if retirement savings are invested in very safe assets, they will not produce a high rate of return. In October 2008, for example, the promised real interest rate on inflation-protected Series I savings bonds was 0%. If these bonds are held for their full thirty-year term, investors will receive a return on their investment that corresponds to the rate of consumer inflation. The purchasing power of the investment will be the same in thirty years as it was on the day the savings bond was issued. Other kinds of savings instruments, like corporate stocks and bonds, offer higher expected returns, but they are not guaranteed to produce a positive or even a zero rate of return after adjusting for inflation.

Advocates of individual accounts often overlook the investment risk inherent in private savings. All private investments are subject to risk. Over long periods of time, investments in the U.S. stock market have outperformed other types of financial investments, including U.S. Treasury securities and corporate bonds. This explains why financial advisors recommend that young and middle-aged workers invest most of their retirement savings in the stock market. But stock returns are highly variable from one year to the next. They are substantially more variable over short periods of time than are the returns on safer assets, like short-term Treasury securities.

Some people mistakenly believe the annual ups and downs in the stock market average out over time, assuring even the unluckiest investor a good return if she invests steadily over a full career. A moment's reflection shows that this cannot be true. From the end of October 2007 to the end of October 2008, the Standard and Poor's composite stock index fell a bit more than 40% after adjusting for changes in the U.S. price level. Shares purchased before November 2007 lost more than four-tenths their value in less than twelve months. For a worker who planned on retiring at the end of 2008, the drop in stock market prices would have required a drastic downsizing of retirement consumption plans if the worker's sole source of income was based on her stock investments.

I have made calculations of the pensions that workers could expect under an individual account plan using information about annual stock and bond returns, interest rates, and inflation dating back to 1872. I start with the assumption that workers enter the workforce at age 22 and work for forty years until reaching their 62nd birthdays. I also assume they contribute 4% of their wages each year to their individual retirement accounts. Wages typically rise through workers' careers until they reach their early or mid fifties, and then earnings begin to fall. When workers reach the age of 62, I assume they use their retirement savings to purchase a single-life annuity. A standard measure of the value of an annuity is the replacement rate, which is simply the amount of the monthly annuity expressed as a percentage of the worker's final wage. (The details and assumptions behind my calculations are spelled out in a note at the end of this chapter.[3])

Figure 3.1 shows replacement rates for workers who invest all their retirement savings in stocks. I track replacement rates for workers retiring at the end of successive years from 1911 through 2008. (To calculate the pension value for someone retiring in 2008, I used information on stock prices, bond yields, and inflation available on October 31, 2008.) The hypothetical experiences of ninety-eight workers are shown in the

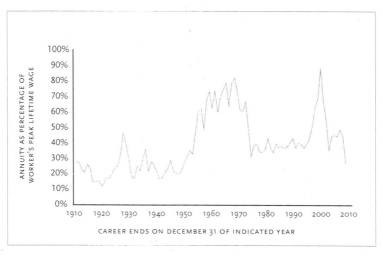

Figure 3.1   Replacement rate obtained from personal account savings of worker who invests solely in stocks and contributes 4% of annual salary over a forty-year career
[Source: Author's calculations based on returns through October 31, 2008.]

chart. The worker who entered the workforce in 1872 and retired at the end of 1911, for example, would have accumulated enough savings in his individual retirement account to buy an annuity that replaced 28% of his peak lifetime earnings (that is, his average earnings between ages 54 and 58). The worker who entered the workforce in 1967 and retired at the end of 2006 could have purchased an annuity that replaced 50% of his peak earnings. The highest replacement rate (89%) was obtained by a worker who entered the workforce at the start of 1960 and retired at the end of 1999. The lowest (12%) was obtained by a worker who began to work in 1881 and retired in 1920. Nine-tenths of the replacement rates shown in the chart fall in the range between 16% and 75%. The average replacement rate is 40%. For workers retiring after 1945, the replacement rate has averaged 49%.

The main lesson to be drawn from the chart is that individual retirement accounts invested solely in the stock market offer a very shaky foundation for a secure retirement income. Workers fortunate enough to retire when stock prices are high obtain big pensions, while workers with the bad luck to retire after markets plunge can be left with a very meager retirement income. The largest pension shown in the chart is

	100% STOCK PORTFOLIO	50% STOCK/ 50% BOND PORTFOLIO	100% BOND PORTFOLIO
1968	83	30	11
1974	32	18	11
1993	38	30	23
1999	89	50	25
2002	36	32	25
2007	45	34	23
2008	27	26	22

Source: Author's calculations based on stock and bond return data and inflation statistics for the period 1930–2008. Estimates of 2008 returns and inflation are based on data through October 31, 2008.

Table 3.1   Replacement rates (percent) under alternative investment strategies for workers who retire at the end of selected years, 1968–2008

more than seven times bigger than the smallest one. Even in the years since 1960, the experiences of retiring workers have differed dramatically. The biggest pension was almost four times the size of the smallest one. In the six years from 1968 to 1974, the replacement rate fell fifty-one percentage points, plunging from 83% to 32% (see table 3.1). In the six years from 1993 to 1999, it jumped fifty-one percentage points, soaring from 38% to 89%. In the ten months after January 2008, the predicted replacement rate dropped eighteen percentage points, falling from 45% to 27%, the lowest replacement rate in more than fifty years.

Social Security pensions have been far more predictable and have varied within a much narrower range. The Chief Actuary of Social Security estimates that workers with an average lifetime earnings profile will receive an inflation-adjusted monthly pension that replaces 42% to 46% of their late-career earnings. Workers with lower-than-average earnings receive higher replacement rates.[4] Compared with most forms of private savings, traditional Social Security provides a more predictable basis for retirement planning and a much more reliable foundation for basic retirement income.

ALTERNATIVE INVESTMENT STRATEGIES

The calculations shown in figure 3.1 refer to the experiences of workers who consistently invest 4% of their wages in U.S. equities. This

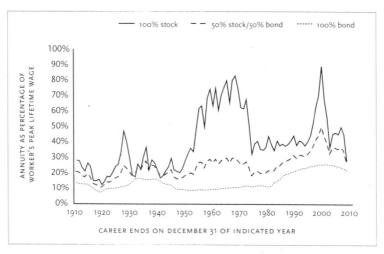

Figure 3.2   Replacement rate obtained from personal account savings of worker who contributes 4% of annual salary over a forty-year career

[Source: Author's calculations based on returns through October 31, 2008.]

investment strategy has on average yielded the best pension available to most U.S. workers. Workers who do not want to accept the risk associated with equity investment can put some or all of their savings in less risky assets, such as corporate or U.S. Treasury bonds. Figure 3.2 shows replacement rates when workers invest part or all of their retirement savings in U.S. government bonds. Under one of the alternative investment strategies, workers place half their savings in long-term government bonds and the other half in stocks. Under the less risky strategy, they invest all their savings in government bonds.

As can be seen in the chart, workers who choose a less risky investment strategy will experience less variability in replacement rates. Between 1999 and 2002, workers who invested everything in stocks saw replacement rates fall 53 percentage points, while workers who invested half their savings in bonds saw replacement rates fall 18 percentage points, and those who invested all their savings in bonds saw the replacement rate fall just 0.1 percentage point. Of course, workers who opt for a low-risk investment strategy will also receive a lower replacement rate on average than they would obtain if they invested all their savings in equities. Whereas the average replacement rate under a 100% stock investment strategy is 40%, the average under the 50% stock / 50% bond strategy is only 24%. Under the 100% government bond strategy, the average is just 14%. Figure 3.2 emphasizes the trade-off between good returns on retirement savings, on the one hand, and uncertainty over the future value of retirement savings, on the other. A worker's retirement income is more predictable and less risky if he invests solely or mainly in very safe assets, but his retirement income is likely to be considerably lower. In many years, workers who adopted the low-risk investment strategy obtained a much lower real rate of return on their individual account savings than on their Social Security contributions.

The uncertainty of individual account pensions is understated in the replacement rate charts for two reasons. First, my calculations do not take account of the effects of inflation in the years after a worker retires. In periods of low inflation, such as the 1950s and the late 1990s, consumer prices were fairly stable. In other periods, including the 1940s, the 1970s, and the early 1980s, inflation was high and erratic. Social Security benefits are adjusted upward to reflect changes in prices, sparing pensioners from the adverse effects of unexpected inflation. Workers with private pensions or annuities do not receive this kind of inflation protection. As a result, private pensioners experience big drops in the purchasing power of their annuities when prices rise unexpectedly.

Investor psychology poses a second kind of risk that is not reflected in the charts. All my calculations are based on the assumption that workers follow a disciplined and consistent investment strategy throughout their careers. Research studies show that many of us are neither consistent nor disciplined in our portfolio choices. We over-invest in assets that have performed strongly in the recent past, and we sell assets after a persistent or sharp fall in prices. These tendencies mean that many of us are inclined to buy assets when their price is high and sell them after their price has declined. Workers who make this kind of investment error will earn lower returns than the returns shown in the charts. The risk that workers might choose a bad investment strategy does not arise in the current Social Security program. Social Security provides a minimally adequate pension for nearly all workers who make contributions over a full career, regardless of each individual worker's investment expertise.

THE BOTTOM LINE

Workers can improve their living standards in old age if they set aside part of their wages in a retirement plan. In fact, as I argue elsewhere in this volume, all wage and salary workers should be offered enrollment in an employer-sponsored retirement plan. If workers want to receive a comfortable income in old age, a large majority should participate in such a plan during most of their careers. Except in the case of workers who have very low lifetime wages, Social Security benefits will not replace even two-thirds of the worker's pre-retirement earnings. For that reason, I see a powerful case for ensuring that all workers have access to either a traditional company pension or a workplace retirement savings plan in order to top up the benefits provided by Social Security. There is a compelling case for designing the employer-based system in such a way that most workers will be eager to participate.

The question is, what kind of basic public retirement plan offers the best guarantee that workers will receive a predictable and minimally adequate income when they retire? As the recent financial turbulence should remind us, the most secure cornerstone for retirement income is a traditional Social Security pension. It replaces a predictable percentage of workers' wages, it is adjusted every year to protect retirees against the risk of inflation, and it is ultimately backed by the taxing authority of the federal government.

The debate over Social Security reform has focused on Social Security's funding problems and the supposed advantages of personal savings accounts in generating high rates of return for contributors. What critics of the current Social Security program often overlook is the problem of financial market risk. The attractions of a personal savings account can seem compelling when investment returns have been consistently high, as was the case in the 1990s. However, this advantage of private savings seems more questionable after there has been a stock market crash or a surge in consumer prices.

The Social Security program has faced only one genuine financial crisis in its sixty-year history. This occurred in the early 1980s, when, as a result of high inflation and a severe recession, the Old-Age and Survivors Insurance Trust Fund was nearly depleted. Congress and President Reagan had to agree on a plan to fix Social Security in order to keep benefits flowing. They adopted a reform package that modestly increased contribution rates, scaled back the after-tax value of benefits, and gradually increased the normal retirement age over the next forty years. Lawmakers did not fundamentally change the essential features of the program. Few people in 1983 thought the program should be scrapped or downsized. Almost no one argued that Social Security should be partly or entirely replaced with a system of private retirement accounts. Policymakers' reluctance to tinker with the basic features of the program is easily explained. In 1983 voters were acutely aware that the value of stocks, bonds, and other forms of personal savings could fall—and fall sharply—without warning. When asset values plummet, retirees and aged workers who rely solely on personal savings to fund their retirement can face a very bleak future. The statistics displayed in figure 3.2 show that, after 1973, workers who invested their retirement savings wholly or partly in the stock market saw a dramatic fall in their expected retirement incomes compared with the incomes they would have received if they retired before 1973.

Few people in the 1930s or early 1980s suffered under the illusion that private retirement accounts offer a secure foundation for old-age income. Recent sell-offs in the stock and bond markets had persuaded most Americans that Social Security was valuable and worth preserving. It is conceivable that the financial market turbulence of the past few years has had the same kind of effect on public opinion. Social Security's long-term funding problem certainly needs to be addressed. But it is hard to argue that the most sensible fix involves scaling back Social Security's basic promises in order to make room for a bigger private savings system.

APPENDIX: INCOME SOURCES OF AMERICANS OVER AGE 65

Income from Social Security is currently the most important source of income for America's aged population. In 2007 it accounted for 39% of the total income received by the elderly (see figure 3.3). Income from pensions other than Social Security is the second most important source of income, accounting for almost one-fifth of the income of the aged. Income from personal savings, mainly derived from interest and dividends, provides 16% of total income.

Social Security benefits are a much more important source of income for aged Americans with limited means (see figure 3.4). In the

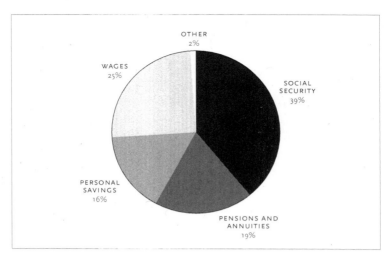

Figure 3.3   Income sources of Americans who are 65 and older: percentage shares (2007)
[Source:Employee Benefit Research Institute tabulations of Census Bureau data files.]

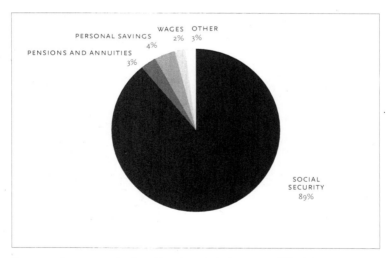

Figure 3.4   Income sources of aged Americans in the bottom one-fifth of the income
distribution (2007)   [Source:Employee Benefit Research Institute tabulations of Census Bureau data files.]

·bottom one-fifth of the income distribution of the elderly, Social Security accounts for almost 90% of total household income. Pensions and
income from personal savings account for a total of 7%.

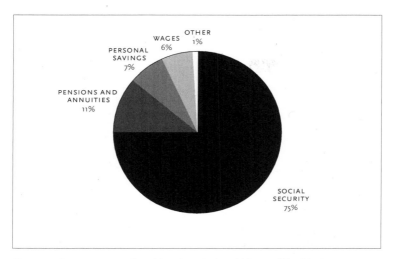

Figure 3.5   Income sources of aged Americans in the middle one-fifth of the income distribution (2007)   [Source: Employee Benefit Research Institute tabulations of Census Bureau data files.]

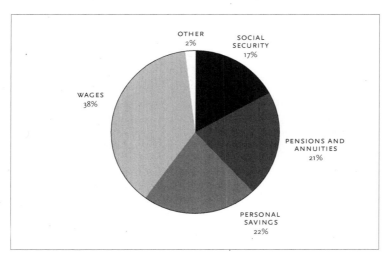

Figure 3.6   Income sources of aged Americans in the top one-fifth of the income distribution (2007)   [Source: Employee Benefit Research Institute tabulations of Census Bureau data files.]

Even in the middle of the income distribution, however, Social Security benefits provide a large fraction of the incomes received by aged Americans (see figure 3.5). Three-quarters of the total income received by the aged in the middle one-fifth comes from a Social Security check. About 18% is derived from an employer pension or personal savings.

In the top one-fifth of the income distribution, Social Security benefits are a much less important source of income for the aged (see figure 3.6). Only about one dollar in six comes from a Social Security check. More than 40% of their income is derived from an employer pension or from household investments in stocks, bonds, bank accounts, and real estate. Many high-income elderly are not yet retired, however. For the high-income aged, almost four-tenths of income comes from wages and self-employment earnings. When the working elderly withdraw altogether from the labor force, a larger percentage of their incomes will come from Social Security. Indeed, Social Security is a more important source of income for the very old, who are very unlikely to work, than it is for the elderly who have just passed age 65.

NOTES

1   According to the government's most recent estimates of the long-term funding shortfall, the Social Security contribution rate would have to increase about 1.7 percentage points — 0.85 percentage points on workers and 0.85 percentage points on employers — if the program is to pay all promised Old-Age, Survivors, and Disability Insurance benefits over the next seventy-five years. The current Social Security contribution rate is 12.4 percentage points, half paid by employees and half paid by employers. See Board of Trustees of OASDI, *The 2008 Annual Report of the Board of Trustees of the Federal Old-Age and Survivors Insurance and Federal Disability Insurance Trust Funds* (Washington, DC: Social Security Administration, 2008); and Joni Lavery, "Social Security Finances: Findings of the 2008 Trustees Report," *Social Security Brief* (National Academy of Social Insurance) 28 (March 2008).

2   There are two problems that make the comparison misleading. First, the claimed return on Social Security contributions is too low. Some contributors will earn negative returns on their Social Security contributions, but on average future returns are expected to be between 1% and 1.5%, even if contributions must be raised or benefits reduced in order to eliminate the program's funding shortfall. Second, workers will not have an opportunity to earn the stock market rate of return on all their retirement contributions, even if Congress establishes an individual account system. Workers' overall rate of return on their contributions to the retirement system will be an average of the return obtained on their contributions to individual accounts and the return earned on their contributions to whatever remains of the

traditional Social Security program. For most people who are currently at work or who will join the workforce in the next three decades, the combined rate of return will be much closer to the current return on Social Security contributions than it will be to 7%.

3   I assume that the age profile of earnings in a given year matches the age profile of earnings for American men in 1995 as reported by the Census Bureau. In addition, I assume that average earnings in the economy as a whole grow 1.5% a year. While it would be interesting to see how workers' pensions would vary if we altered the percentage of contributions invested in exotic assets, in my calculations I assume that all contributions are invested in a combination of U.S. stocks and long-term U.S. government bonds. The total return calculation for stocks is based on the return for the Standard and Poor's composite stock index; the total return calculation for bonds reflects the return on U.S. government debt with a maturity of at least ten years. Interest and dividend payments from the worker's investment portfolio are immediately reinvested, and the worker's portfolio is rebalanced at the end of every year to maintain a constant ratio of stock and bond investments. Optimistically, I assume that workers incur no expenses buying, selling, or holding stocks and bonds. When workers reach their 62nd birthdays, they use their stock accumulations to purchase a single-life annuity for males. (Joint survivor annuities for a worker and a spouse would be about one-fifth lower than the ones shown in the charts.) To determine the annuity company's charge for the annuity, I use the Social Security Actuary's life table for males reaching age 65 in 1995. The annuity company is assumed to invest solely in long-term U.S. government bonds, so when it determines the price of an annuity, it uses the current yield on long-term government bonds. I assume that the annuity company sells a fair annuity. It does not earn a profit, incur administrative or selling costs, or impose extra charges to protect itself against the risk of adverse selection in its customer pool. These assumptions are unrealistic. Annuity companies typically charge an amount that is between 10% and 15% of the selling price of annuities to cover these items. My assumptions therefore yield an overly optimistic estimate of the pension that each worker would receive. For a full explanation of the calculations, see Gary Burtless, "What Do We Know about the Risk of Individual Account Pensions? Evidence from Industrial Countries," *American Economic Review* 93, no. 2 (May 2003): 354–59.

4   Michael Clingman, Orlo Nichols, and Chris Chaplain, "Illustrative Benefits for Retired Workers, Disabled Workers, and Survivors Scheduled Under Current Law," *Actuarial Note* (Office of the Chief Actuary, Social Security Administration) 2008.4 (August 2008): 3.

CHAPTER FOUR

The Plan to Save American Workers' Retirements

TERESA GHILARDUCCI

The inefficiencies and inequity of our employer-based, voluntary, commercial pension system mean that workers in their mid fifties and younger face less retirement income security than their parents and grandparents did.[1] This is a reversal of fortune and the result of flawed policies. Before the Great Depression, the rich used to be the only members of our society who had enough resources and lived long enough to officially retire. But, over time, with a growing American economy, better health, and political resolve, we saw an expansion of Social Security, Medicare, and employer pensions, and all workers could retire with dignity and financial independence. These programs are clever financial institutions that, despite the difficulty inherent in saving, allowed people to have fairly high retirement savings rates before the employer pension system collapsed. This shows that we are not doomed materialists. Americans, with the same basic human nature, had much higher savings rates in the years before the mid 1980s with different sets of retirement savings institutions than we have now.

A prosperous, civilized society such as ours should aim to promote longer lives and the choice to retire. Making pensions universal by requiring employers and workers to contribute 5% of earnings into a retirement account (in addition to the 15.3% combined employer and employee contributions for Social Security and Medicare) and transforming tax expenditures for 401(k) plans into refundable tax credits to pay for these accounts may help to achieve that goal. I propose a progressive system of universal retirement accounts called Guaranteed Retirement Accounts (GRAs).

RETIREMENT SECURITY AND THE
2008 FINANCIAL MARKET CRISIS

In September of 2008, Congress and the president had to react to the modern financial order changing forever. Many people's retirement plans were based on that financial order, and these plans have also changed forever. Never before has the Social Security program's strength in providing security and guaranteed income been so apparent. In September, Social Security recipients enjoyed a 2.3% rise in their benefits; in October, 401(k) holders saw their accounts plunge by 20%.

Even if the stock market recovers and the eventual loss for people who can wait out the recession comes to something less than 20%, there will still be chronic anxiety about retirement security because of the corrosive effects of 401(k)-type plans. 401(k) plans did not expand pension coverage past the 50% of the workforce covered by supplemental pensions since the 1970s, nor did they increase national savings rates. However, 401(k) plans do add to the profits and growth of the financial sector and consume ever-increasing tax expenditures from the U.S. Treasury.

SHORT- AND LONG-TERM SOLUTIONS TO THE RETIREMENT CRISIS

Short term, since 401(k) plans and individual retirement accounts (IRAs) are financial institutions — the "bank" where 38% of the workforce intends to save for their retirement — I propose to let workers voluntarily trade their 401(k) and 401(k)-type plan assets (perhaps valued at mid August prices) for a Guaranteed Retirement Account composed of government bonds (earning a 3% return adjusted for inflation). The Guaranteed Retirement Account will pay an inflation-adjusted annuity, based on the accumulated funds, when the worker collects Social Security.

How would this work? Take a 55-year-old who had $50,000 in his 401(k) account in August and faces job loss and also, sadly, the loss of all hopes of retiring. Let him swap out the $50,000 for a guarantee of $500 per month. (Congress may want to allow a one-time 5% hardship withdrawal.) The economy is in downturn, but a guaranteed income from his former 401(k) removes a source of financial anxiety.

Going forward, I propose that Congress set up universal Guaranteed Retirement Accounts and rearrange the $80 billion of tax subsidies for individual retirement accounts — 401(k)s and IRAs — so that every worker gets $600 in their GRAs every year. 401(k) plans will not disappear or lose all their tax-favored status.

Because there is a long-run retirement crisis, not in Social Security, but in the heavily tax-subsidized, private, and voluntary commercial tier of our nation's pension system, over half of workers will not have enough income after age 65 to replace the bare necessity of 70% of their pre-retirement income (according to Boston College's Retirement Risk Index). Think of retirement income as the food pyramid. Social Security is at the base, like grains and vegetables; the middle tier where the fruits and meat belong is the employer-based system; and up at the top with the whiskey and chocolate are private and personal savings. The crisis is occurring in the top two layers as employer pensions erode and debt swamps personal wealth. It is necessary to expand Social Security's poverty prevention portion by increasing the benefits of the recipients who are living on or near poverty incomes; my proposal reforms the employer-based and savings wealth accumulation portions of our retirement system.

THE PARADOX OF LOW SAVINGS RATES

From the 1990s on, Americans' retirement savings accounts should have been overflowing. Five trends predicted record-high savings rates. First, people with more education save more, and the American workforce has never been more educated. Second, middle-aged workers save more than any other age group, and in 2007 there were an estimated 73 million baby boomers in the United States who were between the ages of 47 and 62. Third, high-income people have higher savings rates, and the richest U.S. households have gained the most income since the 1990s (even though most male workers experienced no real wage gains, the top of the wage distribution did, and that is the group that saves the most). Fourth, the entire nation is richer than ever before, and when people have money, they buy more of what they want — including retirement "leisure." In the 1960s and 1970s, as the economy grew, older people both lived longer and retired earlier.[2] Finally, Congress has expanded tax breaks for retirement savings since the 1980s, so that the value of the favorable tax treatment for retirement savings is at an all-time high.

To be clear, saving is hard. Humans often lack the foresight, discipline, and investing skills required to sustain a savings plan (see Munnell in this volume). But these human weaknesses have always been with us. On the other hand, the decline in retirement savings in the United States is rather recent.

The deep decline in national savings rates showed up in the 1990s when employers started to reduce their contributions into defined benefit pension plans,[3] suggesting that these plans were a main driver of national savings. The expansion of 401(k)-type plans did not boost savings because they supplanted already existing defined benefit plans, were cheaper for the employer, and did not expand pension coverage to people who had no pension plan. This is surprising: although 401(k)-type plans are growing,[4] they do not expand pension coverage. Instead, they replace existing traditional pension plans. When groups of workers who ordinarily do not have pensions get them — poultry workers, janitors, and home-care workers, for example — it is most likely because they are included in a newly negotiated, collectively bargained defined benefit plan. From 1999 to 2005, the correlation between defined benefit coverage growth rates and pension coverage growth rates was 79%, while the correlation between defined contribution and pension coverage growth rates was a negative 10%.[5]

The differences in the characteristics of 401(k) plans and traditional pension plans explain the puzzling and frustrating paradox that national savings fell even though 401(k) plans, and taxpayer subsidies for them, grew. Defined benefit plans are institutionalized, contractual forms of saving that happen automatically at work. Workers have little discretion about whether to save or spend. Workers cannot opt out, decide how much to invest, or readily take out lump-sum payments. Even though 401(k) plans do not increase pension coverage nor secure retirement income, people like their portability and like to watch their individual accounts grow (see Burtless in this volume). People do not like the financial and investment risks, or the risk of outliving their money, inherent in 401(k) accounts. Pension reform must adopt the good features of both the 401(k)-type and defined benefit plans. Saving for retirement must be easy, consistent, adequate, and safe.

Social scientists have argued that competitive consumption makes it hard for people to sacrifice small gratifications for delayed, if large, rewards. But we humans are not hopeless. Economist Robert Frank[6] points out that in forming Social Security and employer pensions, voters essentially created "arms agreements" against competitive acquisition. This good public-policy sense has reversed itself as 401(k) plans have enjoyed a privileged regulatory environment while defined benefit plans have been abandoned.

The paradox—excellent conditions for retirement saving existed while retirement savings eroded—is caused by two factors. The first is that an ineffective and extremely costly tax policy favors the wrong kind of pension plan—the 401(k)-type plan—and two, a realignment of responsibilities and risk-bearing to individuals and families and away from employers and government makes securing retirement income more difficult. These two policy-induced mistakes need to be dealt with and resolved.

THE GROWING FECKLESSNESS OF NATIONAL RETIREMENT INCOME POLICY

Much of our government's spending on retirement security is sneaky. Most people think that Social Security and Medicare are the extent of the federal government's spending on the elderly. Yet this "direct cost" understates the true spending on pensions because the U.S. government uses "tax expenditures"—the value of the tax code's exemption of income for certain activities—to encourage workers and the nation's business owners to spend their income in socially approved ways. American retirement policy is distinguished from many European counterparts by its nurturing of a two-part system. One part is the direct administration of Social Security and other social insurance programs. The other part is indirect and less visible: generous tax breaks for employer- and individual-based plans—401(k)s, IRAs, defined benefit plans, and an alphabet soup of other savings plans. In 2007, Social Security and Medicare cost $800 billion. Tax expenditures for retirement plans—traditional employer pensions (defined benefit plans), 401(k) plans, IRAs, other savings vehicles dedicated for disbursement at older ages, and exemptions of Social Security and other federal pensions from tax—totaled over $156 billion.[7] In 2004, taxes not collected on pension contributions and earnings equaled a fourth of annual Social Security contributions and, at over $114 billion, were perversely larger than household savings of $102 billion.[8] The tax breaks were supposed to expand the proportion of people covered by employer and individual pensions and increase retirement security. They have failed.

One of the reasons the tax breaks do not work is who they help. Since pension tax breaks are deductions from income, high-income earners get more of a break than low-income workers. If a lawyer earning $200,000 makes a $1,000 contribution to his 401(k) plan, he reduces his income tax by $350. If his receptionist, earning $20,000, makes the same $1,000 contribution (which is much less likely), she will save only $150 in taxes. The Brookings Institution and the Urban Institute calculate that the 3% of taxpayers with incomes over $200,000 per year get 20% of the tax subsidies.[9] And, for all this effort, Americans get no extra savings. At most, this complicated system creates economic activity when accountants happily transfer money between taxed accounts to tax-sheltered accounts and taxpayers foot the bill. The value of tax expenditures for 401(k) plans is projected to grow 28% between 2006 and 2009 while the value of tax expenditures for traditional plans is projected to fall by 2.1%.[10] The 2009 tax expenditures for 401(k) plans, IRAs, and Keogh plans (tax-deferred retirement plans for self-employed individuals and unincorporated businesses) are estimated to be $75.1 billion and for defined benefit plans $45.7 billion.

In sum, the shift toward 401(k) plans increases tax expenditures, does little to expand retirement savings, and favors workers who need the help least. All told, the tax subsidies are not meeting a public purpose. The top-heavy benefits for 401(k) plans have proven counterproductive—since 1999, tax expenditures for retirement plans grew by 20% while retirement plan coverage fell. A sharp turn in federal policy to redirect the hundreds of billions of dollars in tax expenditures for retirement plans would help stem the loss of pension security for most American workers.

Comprehensive retirement income security reform aims to reduce the risks faced by participants in the present pension system, which are easy to identify once the 401(k) process is dissected and the mechanics of defined plans are understood. Participants in 401(k)-type plans must successfully execute three steps to secure their retirement — accumulating enough assets, investing the assets well, and drawing from the account appropriately until death. This "do-it-yourself" approach is vulnerable to the tragic consequences of amateurishness. Specifically, we can name these risks: Saving too little and withdrawing before retirement can be lumped into the category of "temptation risk." Twenty percent of workers (even high-income workers) do not participate in the voluntary accounts when offered; 45% of workers cash out or borrow from them before retiring.[11] In 2004, the average size of a 401(k) account for people between 55 and 64 years of age was about $54,000, and the median was $23,000, which would yield an annuity for a 65-year-old of about $50, or $23 per month.[12] In addition, people borrow from their 401(k) plans, reducing the amount of money available for retirement. Even more significantly, half of workers cash out their 401(k) plan accumulations when they leave a job. This makes this portable savings vehicle, ironically, the most inappropriate form of retirement savings for a mobile workforce and cuts across the conventional wisdom that workers want 401(k)s.

"Investment risks" include investing poorly[13] and paying high fees. Administrative fees are — conservatively — estimated to erode over 20% of workers' accumulations.[14] Other investment risks include getting caught in a bear market or inflationary times. Behavioral economists further find that workers rarely diversify enough to reduce risk and maximize return. Since we cannot control the time we live in, the only way to reduce financial risk is to invest in U.S. Treasury bonds that adjust for inflation. However, the rate of return on U.S. Treasury Inflation-Protected Bonds, referred to as TIPS, has not exceeded 3% per year.

Longevity is one of the most intractable risks in any account-based retirement savings strategy. The fear that one will outlive one's retirement money is also the most palpable and scary for older people, especially women. Annuities, such as from defined benefit plans and Social Security, are designed precisely to eliminate longevity risk. Unfortunately, the retail annuity market is very thin even though retirees report being happier when collecting an annuity rather than owning an equivalently valued lump sum.[15] Alicia Munnell and Annika Sundén[16] have some intriguing guesses as to what may be the reason: People avoid annuities because they think they can do a better job investing their lump sums, and they do not want the insurance company to profit from their death. Additionally, people tend to think they will die sooner than they do.[17] Insurance companies are concerned that only people in good health will want annuities, throwing off the participant pool, so they charge high prices for fear of adverse selection. Distrust on both the demand and the supply side of the annuity market means that what people want is not supplied by the market in any meaningful way.[18]

In contrast, defined benefit plans are a form of insurance — employers fund the promise to pay workers a lifelong pension based on years of service. But if a worker leaves the employer without significant pension credits, they subsidize those who do not (see Burtless in this volume). And if the sponsor files for bankruptcy (as has often been the unfortunate case in the airline and steel industries[19]), all benefits may not be insured by the Pension Benefit Guaranty Corporation, so that the worker faces "employment risk" and "employer default risk."[20] See table 4.2 later in this chapter for a compendium of the risks in 401(k)-type plans, defined benefit plans, and Guaranteed Retirement Accounts.

MOTIVES FOR THE EXISTENCE OF 401(K) PLANS

If 401(k) plans are so bad, why are there so many of them? Though workers do not gain much from 401(k) plans, some employers and Wall Street firms do. I followed 700 firms over seventeen years and found that firms that adopted a 401(k) system lowered pension expenses by 3.5 to 5% without sparking worker complaints.[21] Since 401(k) plans are voluntary, many workers (about 20%) who do not bother to contribute are "leaving money on the table" by not accepting the employer match. Employers' contributions are 26% lower than they would be if everyone participated.[22] Employers could pay the match to every worker, as they do under defined benefit plans. Because workers have to trigger the match, and some do not, 401(k) plans boost profits at the expense of retirement income security. Firms find sponsoring 401(k) plans more profitable than sponsoring defined benefit plans. For firms, defined contribution plans are less costly, less risky, and can be funded with their own stock instead of hard cash.

Wall Street firms collect over $40.5 billion annually in 401(k) fees.[23] Yet brokers and human resources often tell workers the fees on their accounts are zero. A good way to see what workers lose when they invest in a 401(k) plan rather than a group-based pension fund is to compare what each earns after fees are subtracted. A comprehensive study by Dutch and Canadian researchers Ron Bauer and Keith Ambachtsheer[24] found that U.S. defined benefit plans—where individuals do not direct their own accounts—earned a 2.66% higher return net of fees on equities than did retail mutual funds. In Canada, the skim was even higher; the retail mutual funds earned 3.16% less. (These are average figures for the twenty-five-year period between 1980 and 2004.) The gap makes sense—investing in retail funds means investors pay for advertising, shareholder profits, and glossy brochures. Add the fact that workers often make the mistake of buying high and selling low, and self-directed accounts earn much less. This is not just a leakage; it is a levee break. Hidden from view, workers are unwittingly transferring huge sums of money to financial firms.

This is bad use of precious dollars accumulated for retirement. 401(k) plans grew not because workers clamored for them but because Congress (encouraged by powerful lobbyists from financial firms) treated 401(k)s as the favored younger child, raising contribution limits and issuing permissive regulations year after year. Meanwhile, the eldest child—defined benefit plans—saw increased regulation.

THE GRA PLAN REDUCES RISKS AND SAVES MONEY

A good pension reform plan incorporates the best features of defined contribution and defined benefit plans. Some hybrid pension plans are available to specialized American groups. Multiemployer plans are found in state and local governments and in the unionized sectors of some industries (for example, construction, coal mining, trucking, textiles, and retail food). These plans allow people to move from one participating employer to another without losing their defined benefit pension plan. The largest defined contribution pension plan on the planet is the Teachers Insurance Annuity Association and College Retirement Equities Fund (TIAA-CREF), the plan for faculty and researchers at universities and related research institutions. TIAA-CREF has defined benefit features—the benefits are paid out in an annuity, and lump-sum withdrawals are very limited.

When the Bush administration promoted personal accounts for Social Security, it hoped to develop a political consensus that Social Security is in serious trouble because people are living longer and the baby boom generation is about to retire. Since defined benefit pensions are an employee benefit of the past and Americans are not saving enough for retirement, the administration hoped that the public would agree that the only realistic solution is to cut Social Security benefits (by raising the retirement age and redirecting revenue to personal accounts). Instead, many groups "fought" back—the labor movement, almost all elected Democrats, the AARP (American Association of Retired Persons) and other retiree groups, women's groups, and religious groups developed another narrative, depicting the Social Security shortfall as fixable and arguing that personal accounts would put many vulnerable groups at risk of poverty in old age.

What emerged is a large group of experts agreeing that the problem has less to do with demographics than with a failure of the system that supplements Social Security—the employer-based retirement plans that enjoy ever-increasing tax benefits. The problem is not that we cannot afford retirement; it is that vast sums are wasted through poorly targeted tax incentives, high fees to financial institutions, and other leakages. The bad news is also the good news: if used correctly, there is more than enough money to secure everyone's retirement.

IMPLEMENTING THE GRA PLAN

Here is what a new president and Congress can do to restore retirement income security. Step one for the government is to reverse the runaway waste in our retirement system. Though we aimed to manipulate the tax code to raise national savings and improve retirement security, both got worse, and we would have made better use of those dollars by throwing them down rat holes (at least the rats could make cozy nests). But Congress only increased those tax breaks when it passed the so-called Pension Protection Act of 2006. The president should immediately replace the tax deductions for 401(k)-type plans with a $600 tax credit deposited into every American worker's retirement account. This would go a long way toward aligning our spending for social insurance with our goals for social insurance. The frustrating reality of disappearing retirement security is that we already spend the amount needed to restore retirement security on programs that purport to do just that. The money is in the Treasury just waiting for a political leadership to rearrange how it is spent.

The second step requires the administration and Congress to address the important division among Americans: between those who do not have access to low-cost, well-run pension accounts and those—including members of Congress, the president, and college professors—who have access to efficient and professional financial advice and pension investment vehicles through defined benefit and defined contribution pension plans in the private and public sector. People are unlikely to decline the opportunity to save money in an account that would guarantee a competitive return and would not charge fees that go to profits, executive salaries, and advertising. Economists Christian Weller and Dean Baker, the Pension Rights Center's "Conversation on Coverage,"[25] and others have called for all Americans to have access to the same type of not-for-profit professional financial institution that is available to federal workers, members of Congress, and the president. All Americans should be able to save in Federal Thrift Savings-like plans.

Steps one and two would be progress, but they are not sufficient. The opt-in, "pretty please" approach using tax deductions and savings incentives doesn't succeed in getting Americans to save voluntarily. Just like all social insurance, efficiency and effectiveness are highest when everyone has to participate. As long as the system is voluntary, options for withdrawal have to exist. But where is the security in that?

Step three, making participation mandatory, must be taken because the voluntary approach is and will always be too expensive and ineffective. Congress should create a Guaranteed Retirement Account system in which workers and employers would each contribute 2.5% of salary (or workers could contribute 5% of payroll) to individual accounts managed by both the Social Security Administration and an investment board made up of professional investors. This board would invest the money in bond and equity markets, creating a large sovereign wealth fund. As in Canada, the trustees would be accountable to Congress.

The government would guarantee each account holder an annual investment return of 3% beyond inflation. The government is the only entity with a long-enough time horizon to guarantee an indexed return that can withstand the ups and downs of financial markets. Since the historical rate of return is closer to 6%, excess returns could be distributed periodically as dividends. Unlike 401(k) accounts, GRAs would have no investment risk, and their administrative costs would be minimal because the contributions would be pooled and run by professionals on a not-for-profit basis. The funds would be mandated and guaranteed, so there would be no advertising. There would still be room for Wall Street; the professional trustees would hire for-profit brokers and financial institutions to invest the funds.

What would be the result? To supplement their Social Security benefits, all workers would have an individual retirement account funded by a $600 contribution from the government as well as worker and employer contributions. People would contribute constantly, not just when they hit the trifecta of working for a firm with a plan, being eligible for the plan, and participating in the plan. The accumulations from consistent 5%-of-pay contributions, earning a 3% real rate of return and being paid as an indexed-annuity at retirement, mean, with Social Security, the average worker will achieve a retirement income that would equal 71% of their prior earnings. The National Retirement Risk Index would be nearly 0%. In addition, every American would have access to a low-fee guaranteed account, meaning that if workers want to save more, they can.

The average American earner, making $39,000 per year, would accumulate $172,300 in a GRA and receive an annuity of $5,800 per year. This is 30% of pre-retirement income. Combined with the Social Security replacement rate of 41%, the average earner would achieve a total replacement rate of 71%! A high earner (with say an annual income of $62,000), because she gets a lower Social Security benefit relative to income, would get a 64% replacement rate, and a low earner (say $17,000 per year) would get a much-needed higher replacement rate of 86%.

Table 4.1 details the GRA outcomes for someone earning an average $38,696 per year, assuming the worker works for forty years and retires at age 65. The projected annuity is based on a 5% contribution rate, a 3% real rate of return, and average life expectancy.

The Guaranteed Retirement Account plan pays for itself by eliminating all tax deductions for contributions to 401(k) plans. It will not increase the federal deficit or require a tax increase. I was shocked by the

	GRA OUTCOMES FOR THE AVERAGE EARNER (EARNING $38,696 PER YEAR)
GRA accumulation for retirement at age 65	$172,291
GRA annuity	$5,795
GRA annuity as a percentage of pre-retirement earnings	30%
Social Security benefits as a percentage of pre-retirement earnings	41%
Total replacement ratio (GRA and Social Security combined)	71%

Source: Teresa Ghilarducci, "Guaranteed Retirement Accounts: Toward Retirement Income Security," *EPI Briefing Paper* (Economic Policy Institute) 204 (November 20, 2007).

Table 4.1   Retirement security under a Guaranteed Retirement Account

math: we can get universal pension coverage and not spend any more than we are spending now. There is so much federal money going to the top that tweaking the distribution frees up a huge amount. According to the Urban Institute and Brookings Institution Tax Policy Center,[26] this savings comes about because employers contribute to the pension plans of the highest earning workers. Seventy percent of government subsidies for retirement accounts go to the top 20% of earners (those earning over $60,000 per year), and 50% of the tax expenditures go to the 6% of workers earning over $100,000 per year (for contributions of up to $20,000 per year). Over 52% of American tax units have earnings less than $40,000. A government tax credit of $600 would therefore pay for 30% of the account balance for the average earner. This would imply moving to middle- and working-class savings accounts 20% of the tax subsidies now going to the top 3%. If we were to allow 401(k) deductions up to $5,000 per year, people would keep their 401(k) plans, the 401(k) vendor world would still thrive, and the system overhaul would cost $25 billion without fixing many of the current pension problems.

ADVANTAGES OF THE GRA PLAN

President Obama can brag that universal pension coverage will require no extra revenue and no additional risk. The Rockefeller Foundation hired a leading private sector actuarial firm to determine if the government, in guaranteeing a 3% real rate of return, would incur substantial risks under the GRA plan, or if promoting a hybrid plan could undermine defined benefit pensions or Social Security. The unpublished report confirmed that the GRA 3% real rate of return was a conservative long-run estimate under a range of plausible investment strategies that a government agency could undertake without any substantial risk of underperforming.[27]

Guaranteed Retirement Accounts provide the best of both the defined benefit and defined contribution worlds by mitigating the risks found in both approaches. With 401(k) plans, there is some risk that employers will not fulfill their promises; the employer establishes an account but contributes on an ad hoc basis and usually contributes only the firm's own stock. On the other hand, these defined contribution accounts are portable and avoid employment risk. With a defined benefit plan, employers promise benefits based on service, so the defined benefit participant bears the employment risk and the risk that the employer may not fund the plan enough due to bankruptcy or some similar business distress.

The GRA account ensures the average worker saves enough — 5% — out of each paycheck. Lump-sum withdrawals (except a small amount at retirement) are not allowed. The accounts are annuitized, and the federal government takes on the investment (and high-fee) risks, financial market risks, and longevity risks. Workers avoid employer-default, employment, and temptation risks, and no longer have to fear spending too much when they are young, losing pension credits, making boneheaded investment mistakes, living during the wrong end of an asset bubble, living too long, or ending up old and in poverty. Table 4.2 compares the risks associated with GRA, defined benefit, and defined contribution plans.

Mandating contributions to a Guaranteed Retirement Account means every worker steadily accumulates assets to fund their golden years, with the federal government's help. The hard-to-see indirect subsidy for retirement savings would turn into a tax credit and retirement contribution of $600 for everyone and actually raise national savings rates and secure Americans' retirement futures.

Whereas the conventional wisdom focuses on increasing voluntary savings and limiting options for early retirement, the GRA plan suggests the opposite: mandating contributions while retaining retirement-age flexibility to reflect differences in health, life expectancy, and other factors. The GRA plan is the only pension reform approach that squarely addresses the issues of adequacy and coverage by requiring that workers

RISK	DEFINED BENEFIT PLAN	DEFINED CONTRIBUTION PLAN/401(K)	GUARANTEED RETIREMENT ACCOUNT PLAN
ACCUMULATION RISKS			
Temptation risks (not saving enough and/or withdrawing funds before retirement)	No	Yes	No
Employment risk	Yes (if the worker leaves at a young age)	No in theory, but yes in fact (workers cash out in job transitions)	No
Employer-default risk	No (if all benefits insured by PBGC)	Not much (unless the account holds substantial employer stock)	No
INVESTING RISKS			
Financial market risk	Not much	Yes	No (3% real rate of return guaranteed)
Investment mistakes risk	No	Yes	No
PAYOUT RISKS			
Longevity risk	No (if no lump-sum payout)	Yes (borrowing from the account or cashing it out instead of rolling it over)	No (mandated annuity except for 10% lump-sum payout at retirement)
Inflation risk	Yes	Yes	No

Table 4.2   A risk comparison: defined benefit, defined contribution, and GRA plans

are covered and contribute a steady 5% of payroll. The GRA plan prevents lopsided subsidies by redirecting tax incentives that benefit only top earners. The GRA plan also encourages — but does not force — later retirement because benefits accrue steadily for every hour of work.

Universal coverage eliminates the adverse selection problem — people who need the insurance the most are the ones who buy it — that, combined with the complexity inherent in choosing among investment products, makes it difficult for individuals to insure against longevity risk by buying annuities. The GRA plan is also responsive to broader labor market trends. While there has been a much-noted decline in the average male retirement age, more women of all ages are working longer. The retirement literature tends to focus on the former trend and not the latter. The "average retirement age" can be a misleading statistic when there are significant changes in labor force participation since what matters is total household years of paid work relative to years in retirement.

In many ways, the GRA plan is a conservative one. It is fully advance-funded, does not increase the government deficit, maintains a strong link between work and benefits, and only provides the bare minimum needed for retirement—the GRA plan will not provide adequate replacement rates if Social Security replacement rates fall below 2008 levels.

A POLITICAL OPENING FOR MANDATORY RETIREMENT SAVINGS

Workers are catching on; surveys show people are worried about affording retirement, and they want the government to help. In 2006, HSBC Bank asked 21,000 workers in twenty nations what the government should do about the expense of aging societies. The answer was a bit surprising. On average, workers preferred compulsory savings to any other policy. A third of Americans wanted the government to force them to save more for retirement; 21% said they prefer an increase in the retirement age; 16% would support a tax increase; and only 9% wanted the government to reduce benefits.[28] In October 2007, a whopping 91% of Americans told a *Wall Street Journal* poll that the government should do something to secure retirement, and 41% said they were not hearing enough from the presidential candidates about retirement income issues.[29]

Americans are seeking financial safe haven as a recession looms large. In the wake of two burst asset bubbles—the tech bubble in 2001 and the housing bubble starting in 2007—and the dismantling of the postwar social compact that brought health and retirement benefits to the middle class in the 1950s and 1960s, Americans are becoming acutely aware of new income risks.[30] Plummeting home prices and an impending recession exacerbate the longer-term and broader problem of Americans' growing economic insecurity. A recession is likely to reduce 401(k) contributions and increase leakages. Fidelity Investments, for example, has already reported an increase in hardship withdrawals and loans. This may not just be the effect of the economic slowdown but also of falling home prices, which limit the availability of home equity withdrawals.

In the retirement arena, Americans are increasingly exposed to financial, longevity, and inflation risks. Individual investors would welcome a guaranteed, low-fee, inflation-indexed place to invest their money. And when it comes to retirement, all retirees want a secure and steady flow of income. The GRA system performs the same pooling function as traditional pension funds, with the government taking over the pension fund's role in smoothing investment returns over time and across generations to pay a guaranteed high-interest annuity.

Furthermore, as the nation undergoes a political realignment, we are beginning to critically assess quasi-free-market solutions that rely on more and more tax breaks and tax cuts. "Big government" may not be attractive, but "smart government" makes sense. The GRA plan addresses voters' concerns about affordability and prudent fiscal spending because the retirement accounts are advance funding. They could be funded with shared employer-employee contributions and entail a revenue-neutral reallocation of government subsidies. Importantly, the plan is designed to minimize the risk of a shortfall requiring a government bailout.

Although most retirement experts — including members of both the conservative Heritage Foundation and the centrist Hamilton Project (an initiative founded by former Clinton Treasury Secretary and Wall Street insider Robert Rubin)[31] — agree that 401(k)s are severely flawed, they have convinced themselves that anything other than an individual savings solution is politically unrealistic. Consequently, they focus on narrow reform such as auto enrollment — requiring workers to opt out of 401(k) plans rather than opting in — as the way to increase retirement savings. Not coincidentally, auto enrollment fits squarely with the agenda of the mutual fund industry. But the financial companies that serve institutional investors will be well served as American workers build up a sovereign wealth fund to pay for GRAs. The broker dealers may lobby against the GRA plan, but private equity firms and large institutions, like State Street Corporation, may welcome them.

The Guaranteed Retirement Account plan has already begun changing the way Washington thinks about retirement. Just recently, in the late fall of 2007, law professor Jon Forman and economist Adam Carasso published a plan very similar to the GRA, using the Carter Commission's name — Mandatory Universal Pension System.[32] (Unfortunately, I believe that their 3% contribution rate doesn't go far enough.) David Walker, former director of the U.S. Government Accountability Office and now president of the conservative Peter G. Peterson Foundation, supports mandatory savings. Members of Congress are also exploring GRAs.

CONCLUSION

For the GRA plan to move forward, opinion leaders and the public need to gain a better understanding of the real challenges we face and how ineffective the tax expenditures for pensions are. Social Security is not the problem; even if no steps are taken to fix the Social Security funding gap, benefits will be unaffected for several decades, and young workers will still have higher benefits than those of current retirees. The over $100 billion currently spent on pension tax expenditures offers an opportunity once Americans understand the situation: they receive little or no government help in saving for retirement, while the bulk of 401(k) tax breaks goes to people at the top of the income distribution who need the help the least. These lessons are important as the next administration moves ahead on comprehensive reform.

The best way to get out of a hole is to stop digging. There is no gold to be found in the pursuit of the argument that Social Security cannot be fixed; it can, and without regressive benefit cuts. Furthermore, defined benefit pensions are not gone. They are important in the public, and some parts of the private, sector. We need to reform the strategy of paying people to save through the flawed 401(k) system. At a bare minimum, we need to make the disclosure of 401(k) fees and the conversion of regressive tax breaks to refundable tax credits preconditions for expanding 401(k) savings and subsidies through auto enrollment. If not, 401(k) plans, with all their shortcomings, will become even more entrenched. Nips and tucks will not transform the 401(k) system into an effective or efficient retirement policy. We need to admit to the limits of a voluntary employer-based system and adopt a hybrid comprehensive solution like Guaranteed Retirement Accounts.

NOTES

1   Good references for the erosion of retirement income security include Frank A. Fernandez and Kyle L. Brandon, "Retirement Savings: By the Numbers," *SIA Research Reports* (Securities Industry Association) 7, no. 7 (June 27, 2006); Christian Weller and Edward N. Wolff, *Retirement Income: The Crucial Role of Social Security* (Washington, DC: Economic Policy Institute, May 2005); Barbara A. Butrica, Howard M. Iams, and Karen E. Smith, "It's All Relative: Understanding the Retirement Prospects of Baby-Boomers," CRR WP 2003-21 (working paper, Center for

Retirement Research at Boston College, November 2003); Laurence Thompson, "Paying for Retirement: Sharing the Gain," in *In Search of Retirement Security: The Changing Mix of Social Insurance, Employee Benefits, and Individual Responsibility*, ed. Teresa Ghilarducci, Van Doorn Oms, John L. Palmer, and Catherine Hill (New York: Century Foundation Press, 2005), chap. 7; and Alicia H. Munnell, Anthony Webb, and Luke Delorme, "A New National Retirement Risk Index," *Issue in Brief* (Center for Retirement Research at Boston College) 48 (June 2006).

2   Teresa Ghilarducci, *When I'm Sixty-Four: The Plot Against Pensions and the Plan to Save Them* (Princeton, NJ: Princeton University Press, 2008), chap. 1.

3   Barry Bosworth and Lisa Bell, "The Decline in Saving: What Can We Learn from Survey Data?" CRR WP 2005-15 (working paper, Center for Retirement Research at Boston College, December 2005).

4   401(k)-type plans are defined contribution plans and include the following: 401(k) plans (about 80% of defined contribution participants); profit-sharing plans; money purchase plans; individual retirement accounts; and 403(b) plans, which are 401(k) plans for employees in the public sector.

5   Teresa Ghilarducci, *Future Retirement Income Security Needs Defined Benefit Pensions*, Report (Center for American Progress, 2006), http://www.americanprogress.org/kf/defined_benefit_layout.pdf. Because they are designed to meet a social goal, there are always conditions on tax breaks. When the federal income tax was implemented in 1913, employer pension contributions were given special tax treatment only if the managerial plans included most of the rank and file. This is in direct acknowledgement that the tax breaks were targeted to the wealthy. The wrangling—over how many tax breaks higher-income employees get in exchange for how many lower-paid workers get employer pension plans—continues to this day and is part of a healthy process of assessing if the tax breaks have the intended effects. Back in 1981, Congress rejected the Carter Commission's call to reconsider the social value of these tax breaks and create a mandatory universal pension system (MUPS). Instead, Congress satisfied the lobbyists for executives and made way for 401(k) plans by creating a section of the tax code that allowed workers to save, pretax, in plans at work. After Wall Street firms and consultants successfully marketed 401(k) plans, the rest—to use a shop-worn phrase—is a history we all know: 401(k)-type plans replaced traditional defined benefit pensions. Over 63% of pensions are defined contribution plans; whereas, in 1975, most pensions were defined benefit plans.

6   Robert H. Frank and Phillip J. Cook, *The Winner-Take-All Society* (New York: The Free Press, 1995).

7   Joint Committee on Taxation, *Estimates of Federal Tax Expenditures for Fiscal Years 2007–2011,* report prepared for the House Committee on Ways and Means and the Senate Committee on Finance, 110th Cong., 1st sess., 2007, Joint Committee Print JCS-3-07.

8   For this provocative insight, see Elizabeth Bell, Adam Carasso, and C. Eugene Steuerle, "Retirement Saving Incentives and Personal Saving," *Tax Facts* (Tax Policy Center, December 20, 2004), http://www.urban.org/retirement_policy/url.cfm?ID=1000739.

9   This is a good paper on the distributional effects of the tax expenditures for defined contribution plans: Leonard E. Burman, William G. Gale, Matthew Hall, and Peter R. Orszag, "Distributional Effects of Defined Contribution Plans and Individual Retirement Accounts," TPC DP 16 (discussion paper, Tax Policy Center, August 2004).

10   Employee Benefit Research Institute, "Tax Expenditures and Employee Benefits: Estimates from the FY 2009 Budget," *Facts from EBRI* (February 2008).

11   For an excellent review of the reasons 401(k)s fail, see Alicia H. Munnell and Annika Sundén, *Coming Up Short: The Challenge of 401(k) Plans* (Washington, DC: Brookings Institution Press, 2004).

12   Munnell and Sundén, *Coming Up Short.*

13   The allocation of assets in a retirement portfolio and the level of administrative and investment fees can crucially affect overall return and risk in a pension plan. When 401(k) plans were first offered, employers that sponsored these pension plans invested the assets for the workers in the plan, providing them with very little choice of investment vehicles. Then there came a trend toward providing workers the opportunity to select among many different kinds of investment vehicles — according to one study, sometimes up to fifty-six choices. We all know to diversify, which workers did when faced with choices. Participants would distribute their contributions evenly across vehicles when there were fewer than five choices, but that tendency changed as the number of choices expanded.

14   Walter Hamilton, Kathy M. Kristof, and Josh Friedman, "Fees Eat Away at Employees' 401(k) Nest Eggs," *Los Angeles Times,* April 23, 2006, http://www.latimes.com/business/la-fi-retire23apr23,0,6166250,full.story?coll=la-home-headlines; and Christian E. Weller and Shana Jenkins, *Building 401(k) Wealth One Percent at a Time: Fees Chip Away at People's Retirement Nest Eggs,* Report (Center for American Progress, 2007), http://www.americanprogress.org/issues/2007/03/pdf/401k_report.pdf.

15   Keith A. Bender and Natalia A. Jivan, "What Makes Retirees Happy?" *Issue in Brief* (Center for Retirement Research at Boston College) 28 (February 2005).

16   Munnell and Sundén, *Coming Up Short.*

17 Ghilarducci, *When I'm Sixty-Four*, 320n26.

18 George A. (Sandy) Mackenzie, *Annuity Markets and Pension Reform* (New York: Cambridge University Press, 2006).

19 Ghilarducci, *When I'm Sixty-Four*.

20 A worker who stays fewer than five years usually earns no credits toward a pension. "Employment risk" alludes to the risk that a worker will leave employment with a firm before vesting or building up significant pension credits. The employment risk under 401(k)-type pension plans is that people take the money out to cover unemployment expenses. And over 40% of 401(k) assets are invested in employer stock, whereas the 1974 Employee Retirement Income Security Act allows defined benefit assets to only hold up to 10% of employer stock. Employers do pose some risk to defined contribution participants. Employers could stop or shrink their 401(k) contribution matches — many employers reduced or stopped matches during the 2001 recession.

21 Teresa Ghilarducci and Wei Sun, "How Defined Contribution Plans and 401(k)s Affect Employer Pension Costs," *Journal of Pension Economics and Finance* 5 (2006): 175–96.

22 To get participation rates, average contribution levels by earnings, and the distribution of employees by earnings, I used information from Munnell and Sundén, *Coming Up Short*. I calculated from the 2003 CPS to make the $3 billion estimate. The average savings per worker is $156 — calculated for their sample of over 800 employees in one firm, the employer saved over $250 per older worker who did not participate in the 401(k) plan even when they were eligible. See also James J. Choi, David I. Laibson, and Brigitte C. Madrian, "$100 Bills on the Sidewalk: Suboptimal Investment in 401(k) Plans," NBER W11554 (working paper, National Bureau of Economic Research, August 2005). Fidelity's *2004 Annual Report* documents employers' match behavior.

23 There are $2.7 trillion in 401(k) assets. The average fee is over $700 per year and average fees are 1.5% of assets, which equals $40.5 billion. See Employee Benefit Research Institute, "401(k) Plan Asset Allocation, Account Balances, and Loan Activity" (information sheet, EBRI, October 23, 2007), http://www.ebri.org/pdf/InfSheet.QDIA.23Oct07.Final.pdf.

24 Keith Ambachtsheer and Rob Bauer, "Losing Ground," *Canadian Investment Review* 20, no. 1 (Spring 2007): 8–14.

25 Similar proposals that expand access to public financial institutes for retirement savings include Dean Baker, "Universal Voluntary Accounts: A Compromise Retirement Solution," Center for American Progress, March 19, 2004, http://

www.americanprogress.org/issues/2004/03/b38731.html; and Dean Baker, *Pensions for the Twenty-First Century*, Report (The Century Foundation, 1999).

26 A Tax Policy Center analysis of the GRA plan found that eliminating 401(k) tax breaks — which only benefit some workers — would free up sufficient funds to pay for $800 refundable tax credits to all workers under the GRA plan, reflecting the enormous cost of these tax breaks. The analysis also found that due to the regressive structure of 401(k) tax breaks, 58% of taxpayers would be better off with a revenue-neutral conversion of 401(k) tax breaks into GRA tax credits, and only 16% of taxpayers would be worse off, most of them in the top income quintile.

27 For calculations, see Teresa Ghilarducci, "Guaranteed Retirement Accounts: Toward Retirement Income Security," *EPI Briefing Paper* (Economic Policy Institute) 204 (November 20, 2007).

28 HSBC, "How should governments finance ageing populations," news release, April 26, 2006, http://www.hsbc.com/1/PA_1_1_S5/content/assets/retirement/2006_for_news_release_final.pdf; and HSBC, *The Future of Retirement: What People Want*, Report (HSBC, 2007), http://www.hsbc.com/1/PA_1_1_S5/content/assets/retirement/2006_for_report_people.pdf (accessed February 2, 2007).

29 Beckey Bright, "Americans See a Dim Outlook For Social Security, Poll Finds," WSJ.com (November 17, 2007), http://online.wsj.com/article/SB119500312722492114.html?mod=pj_main_hs_coll.

30 Jacob S. Hacker, *The Great Risk Shift: the Assault on American Jobs, Families, Health Care, and Retirement and How You Can Fight Back* (Oxford: Oxford University Press, 2006).

31 David John from the Heritage Foundation and Mark Iwry from the Retirement Security Project (sponsored by the Hamilton Project) have proposed automatic individual retirement accounts. The proposal is explained most recently in their testimony to the United States Senate: David C. John and J. Mark Iwry, *Strategies to Reduce Leakage in 401(k)s and Expand Saving Through Automatic IRAs: Hearing on Protecting and Strengthening Retirement Savings*, Senate Special Committee on Aging, 110th Cong., 2d sess., July 16, 2008.

32 Jonathan Barry Forman and Adam Carasso, "Tax Considerations in a Mandatory Universal Pension System" (paper presented at Re-Envisioning Retirement in the 21st Century, Society of Actuaries, May 3–4, 2006), http://www.soa.org/library/monographs/retirement-systems/re-envisioning-retirement/m-as06-2_abstract-VIII.pdf.

CHAPTER FIVE

Learning from International Experience

MITCHELL A. ORENSTEIN

The previous chapters of this book explore what sorts of pension reforms would be best for the United States by looking at the evolution of the U.S. pension system, its problems, and possible solutions. This chapter draws lessons from other countries. Because the problems faced by retirement systems in the United States are similar to those in countries worldwide — an aging population, increased stress on Social Security-type programs, the prospect of inadequate benefits, and employer-based systems that fail to address the needs of all workers — we have an opportunity to learn from the rest of the world.

During the 1990s and the early twenty-first century, the U.S. government avoided major changes in Social Security and expanded tax breaks tied to individual and employer-based pensions. While in the past workplace pensions were primarily defined benefit systems, today they are increasingly based on 401(k)-type individual pension savings accounts. As previous chapters have shown, this policy approach appears insufficient. Social Security remains in need of reform. And 401(k)-type pensions have failed to live up to their promise. Despite the increased amounts of money flowing into the system, they have failed to provide enough benefits to enough people to make up for the emerging shortfalls in Social Security. U.S. policymakers are now searching for alternative methods of fixing the U.S. pension system.

International experience can provide inspiration for U.S. reform. In particular, the United States has much to learn from countries that have sought to reshape the balance between Social Security and individual pension savings accounts. This chapter explores the trend towards individual pension savings accounts in countries worldwide and examines the different routes taken to reform. While taking a global perspective, I show that the United States ultimately has the most to learn from other English-speaking countries with similar social policy traditions and similar levels of Social Security spending and benefits.

SOCIAL SECURITY PRIVATIZATION AND ITS ALTERNATIVES

Many countries have responded to emerging pressures on Social Security by partially or fully replacing Social Security-type programs with systems based on individual pension savings accounts. Middle-income developing countries from Argentina and Chile to Poland and Hungary have confronted growing Social Security liabilities in this way.[1] President George W. Bush advocated this approach for the United States as well. Social Security privatization enables governments to reduce the public burden of future Social Security deficits and shift responsibility for retirement income to individuals. Interestingly, however, only two developed countries have taken this route to reform: the United Kingdom in 1986 and Sweden in 1994. And the United Kingdom has subsequently changed course. At the same time, a growing number of developed countries have adopted a different approach to reform. These countries have not replaced or cut back their Social Security programs, but rather expanded pension savings by making their preexisting employer pension systems mandatory. Australia, Denmark, the Netherlands, New Zealand, and Switzerland have followed this path.[2] The United Kingdom is considering similar reforms. This approach may prove more relevant for the United States than Social Security privatization because of the distinctive features of the U.S. pension system.

THE PROS AND CONS OF SOCIAL SECURITY PRIVATIZATION

When George W. Bush proposed privatizing Social Security in 2005 to enable individuals to divert money to their own individual pension savings accounts, he was introducing a reform to the United States that had already been enacted in more than thirty countries worldwide. Under this approach, countries reduce the amount of money flowing into the Social Security program and divert payroll taxes to individual pension savings accounts. Cutting Social Security benefits and increasing reliance on individual accounts helps to address long-term fiscal problems in aging societies. Many Republican lawmakers continue to advocate a voluntary "carve-out" of the U.S. Social Security program.

The benefits to governments of such a strategy are clear. First, carving out Social Security to fund individual accounts does not require increasing taxes, often one of a politician's least favorite activities. Second, cutting Social Security reduces the government's pension liabilities and relieves budgetary pressure over the long run. Third, introducing individual pension accounts enables the government to reduce pension benefits without people realizing it. Since people cannot calculate the value of their future pension benefits in an individual account, they do not realize that a decline in benefits often accompanies the introduction of such accounts. Fourth, individual accounts address the demographic issue by making people save for their own retirements rather than relying on future (and possibly smaller) generations of workers. Fifth, they shift management of the pension system from the public to the private sector, which helps powerful financial sector constituencies.[3]

However, shifting to a system of individual pension savings accounts presents problems too. Primary among them is the privatization of risk. Governments are happy to get Social Security risk off their books, but shifting this risk to individuals does not make retirement incomes more secure. Individuals become subject to the risks of bad investment decisions, high fees, poor market conditions, and low earnings. Long periods spent in unemployment, study, or unpaid home-care work reduce the ability to pay for retirement. In individual pension savings account systems, workers with high salaries and long, consistent work periods do better. Others do worse. Individual pension accounts provide purely income-related benefits; there is no redistribution between accounts. Therefore, these systems are often paired with a scaled-down Social Security program or state-guaranteed minimum benefits.

The shift to individual pension savings accounts also costs the government money in the short and medium run since payroll tax contributions are diverted away from Social Security, yet Social Security must continue to pay current beneficiaries. Normally, the government must borrow an amount equivalent to the total contributions to individual accounts to finance the Social Security program through the transition. This creates a large "transition cost" deficit that can prove a sizeable fiscal burden.

A further problem is the administrative costs of individual pension savings account systems. Social Security programs are very cheap to administer, but the large number of competing funds in individual account systems tends to drive up costs. This can translate into substantial reductions in retirement benefits, especially for the first generation enrolled, which must finance the administrative costs of setting up the new system during a period of relatively low balances.

INTERNATIONAL MODELS OF PRIVATIZATION

Countries that have carved out their Social Security programs to make way for individual pension savings account systems have done so in three distinct ways. Some countries have entirely eliminated Social Security and "replaced" it with individual pension accounts. The pioneer of the "replacement" model was Chile, which eliminated its Social Security-based system in 1981. People who had contributed to Social Security in the past were given a government bond corresponding to the size of their contributions; this was deposited in their individual account. When balances in many private accounts proved inadequate, Chile passed a new reform in 2007 that increased the level of minimum benefits guaranteed by the state. State-guaranteed minimum benefits are a common feature of replacement-type reforms since many workers fail to accumulate sufficient savings.

Other countries have implemented mandatory, but partial, carveouts of Social Security. In this model of reform, the government requires all employees below a certain age (and their employers) to divert part of their Social Security contribution to individual accounts. Another part continues to be directed to a scaled-back Social Security program. This type of reform has been popular in central and eastern European countries, such as Poland and Hungary, which have long histories of Social Security, large and relatively generous workplace pension systems, and rapidly aging populations. While it is early to evaluate the results of these

SOCIAL SECURITY REPLACEMENT	MANDATORY CARVE-OUT	VOLUNTARY CARVE-OUT
Chile 1981	Sweden 1994	United Kingdom 1986
Bolivia 1997	China 1998	Peru 1993
Mexico 1997	Hungary 1998	Argentina 1994
El Salvador 1998	Poland 1999	Colombia 1994
Kazakhstan 1998	Costa Rica 2001	Uruguay 1996
Dominican Republic 2001	Latvia 2001	Estonia 2001
Nicaragua 2001	Bulgaria 2002	Lithuania 2002
Kosovo 2001	Croatia 2002	
Nigeria 2004	Macedonia 2002	
Taiwan 2004	Russia 2002	
	Slovakia 2003	
	Romania 2004	
	Uzbekistan 2004	

Source: Mitchell A. Orenstein, *Privatizing Pensions: The Transnational Campaign for Social Security Reform* (Princeton, NJ: Princeton University Press, 2008).

Table 5.1   Pension reform worldwide

programs, they have generally reduced retirement benefits overall, as the cuts in Social Security are often deeper than the benefits provided by individual accounts.

A third group of countries lets individuals choose to either divert part of their taxes to an individual account or stay in the Social Security program. This variant is what George W. Bush proposed for the United States in 2005. It is widely regarded as the easiest to sell politically since it allows individuals to choose whether or not to contribute to individual accounts. Countries that adopt voluntary carve-outs often do so because they experience serious political opposition to mandatory reform. Making contributions voluntary can allay the concerns of reform opponents.

Table 5.1 lists those countries that have reformed their Social Security-based pension systems in order to divert funds to individual pension savings accounts, grouped by privatization model.

What is immediately apparent from this table is how few wealthy developed countries have followed any of these privatization approaches to pension reform. Most reforming countries are middle-income developing countries in Latin America and central and eastern Europe. There are three likely reasons for this.[4] First, the World Bank-led transnational campaign to spread individual pension savings accounts has most directly affected the Bank's own clients — middle-income developing countries. Second, many of the early reformers were in Latin America, where they were influenced by the Chilean model. Third, developed countries are slower to reform for political reasons. Interest groups and policy communities tend to be more powerful in developed countries and capable of preventing reforms that go against their interests. In addition, well-functioning democracies in the developed world — as they are meant to do — provide greater opportunities to influence the policy process. Finally, it tends to be harder for countries with larger Social Security programs to enact reform. All these factors help to explain why the partial or full replacement of Social Security with individual accounts has proceeded more rapidly in middle-income developing than in developed countries.

THE TRANSNATIONAL CAMPAIGN
FOR SOCIAL SECURITY REFORM

One reason why developing countries have carved out their Social Security-based systems more readily is that they were influenced by a transnational campaign for Social Security reform during the 1990s and the early twenty-first century.[5] This campaign was shaped both by a privatization pioneer and the largest and most influential organization pushing pension privatization — Chile and the World Bank.

Under military dictator General Augusto Pinochet in the early 1980s, Chile undertook radical economic reforms led by the so-called Chicago Boys, a group of young economists trained at leading U.S. universities.[6] Pinochet called on these economists to design various economic reforms, including a pension reform that replaced the previous Social Security-based system with one based on individual pension savings accounts. The Chilean model excited much interest in other countries in Latin America. However, its association with the Pinochet regime tarnished the model's reputation, particularly among the political left.

After a period of poor economic performance in the mid 1980s, Chile's economy began to improve dramatically, and other Latin American countries began to seriously consider its pension reform model. Observers began to believe that the accumulation of pension funds in individual accounts had created a new pool of domestic capital for investment, which was helping to spur economic growth. At the same time, major international organizations like the World Bank, the Inter-American Development Bank, the UN Economic Council for Latin America, and others began to support pension reform.[7] They were joined by Chilean reformers and pension fund managers, who organized international conferences to promote the Chilean model and acted as consultants throughout Latin America and beyond.[8]

In 1994, the World Bank published *Averting the Old Age Crisis*, marking a second pivotal moment in the transnational campaign for Social Security reform. This volume, which strongly endorsed mandatory systems of individual pension savings accounts, presented a more flexible approach to including private pension savings accounts as part of national pension systems. Whereas Chile completely replaced its Social Security-based pension system, the World Bank advocated instead mandatory carve-outs: diverting only a portion of Social Security revenues to individual accounts while maintaining a scaled-down Social Security program.

Backed by comprehensive research and powerful figures in the international economics community, such as Lawrence Summers, Chief Economist of the World Bank, *Averting the Old Age Crisis* quickly became a template for World Bank policy advice. The economists who participated in the drafting of the report formed the core of a World Bank pension reform advisory group that transferred the World Bank model to countries worldwide. The World Bank successfully recruited other organizations to partner with its efforts, particularly regional development banks such as the Inter-American Development Bank and the Asian Development Bank. Next, the World Bank developed a strong relationship with the bilateral U.S. Agency for International Development (USAID), which saw pension privatization as part of its fiscal sector reform strategy for Central and Eastern European transition states.[9] The Organization for Economic Cooperation and Development also supported efforts to promote pension reforms among and beyond its member states, as did many Chilean, Latin American, and European policy entrepreneurs. With this powerful coalition of transnational actors at its side, the World Bank extended the reach of its advisory capacity and divided the task of spreading reform worldwide.

Starting in the early 1990s, pension privatization plans inspired by the Chilean replacement model and the World Bank's multi-pillar model spread to more than thirty countries around the world. Most of these countries have been concentrated in two regions: Latin America and central and eastern Europe. Pension privatization spread from Chile to Latin America in the early and mid 1990s and then, starting in 1998, to central and eastern Europe, with extensive support from the World Bank, USAID, and their partners. Many African, Asian, and Middle Eastern countries began to seriously consider pension privatization plans in the late 1990s and into the twenty-first century thanks to the World Bank Institute organizing numerous seminars to promote new pension reform ideas in these regions.[10]

In Africa, Nigeria became the first adopter in 2004; South Africa was in the process of considering reforms in 2007.[11] Taiwan's adoption of the new pension reforms in 2004 signaled their increasing prevalence in Asia as well. China adopted reform legislation in 1998, but implementation has been slow and spotty. Other Asian countries are currently considering mandatory individual pension savings accounts. It is difficult to know how well new individual account systems are working because they do not pay out benefits for many years. However, some of the early countries in this reform wave have experienced problems. Chile found that accumulations were insufficient to fund retirement for lower income workers and has had to increase minimum state-financed pension payments. In the midst of the 2008 global financial crisis, Argentina nationalized individual pension savings accounts to fill a hole in its Social Security budget.

WHY LESS REFORM IN DEVELOPED COUNTRIES?

While many middle-income developing countries have reformed their pension systems through privatization, the United Kingdom and Sweden are the only developed countries so far to have carved out their Social Security programs to introduce individual pension savings accounts. The United Kingdom's 1986 reforms are the most similar to what President Bush proposed for the United States in 2005. The United Kingdom, like the United States, has a relatively small Social Security program. In the early 1980s, Prime Minister Margaret Thatcher pushed forward with reforms that enabled people to opt out of part of their Social Security pension and divert their contributions to individual pension savings accounts. While the Thatcher reforms were bold, they have not been emulated elsewhere because of a long and expensive controversy over the "mis-selling" of these accounts and the costs that they ultimately imposed. The insurance and fund management companies that managed these private pensions convinced many Britons to switch into individual accounts, even when their benefits would have been predictably higher by staying within their existing state or occupational pension system. Eventually, fund providers were forced to compensate their clients to the tune of 11 billion pounds (around $20 billion). In addition, because individuals were allowed to return to the state pension system at any point, the shift to individual pension savings accounts did not save the government any money. Instead, the Thatcher reforms cost the government an estimated 10 billion pounds. Later governments were forced to clean up the pension mess that the Thatcher government left behind.[12]

Sweden's pension reform has been more successful. Sweden has a larger Social Security program,[13] and in 1994 a new conservative government created a new working group, composed of representatives of all the major political parties and trade unions, to carve out a small part of the program and introduce a carefully regulated system of individual pension savings accounts. The Swedish accounts are unique. Rather than being marketed to directly (as in the United Kingdom), individuals inform the government which funds they have selected, and a government agency directs their contributions to those funds. Fund companies do not know who their clients are, thus they cannot mis-sell their products using high-pressure sales tactics. With many precautions in place to prevent mis-selling and other problems, the Swedish reform has worked well, but it represents a relatively small proportion of the country's overall pension system. While 16% of payroll goes to the Social Security program, only 2.5% goes to individual accounts.

The governments of many developed countries — often but not always right-wing governments — have considered carving out part of their Social Security programs to make room for a system of mandatory individual pension savings accounts. President George W. Bush proposed such a reform for the United States in 2005 but was unable to get legislation passed. Except for the United Kingdom and Sweden, no developed countries have adopted mandatory pension savings accounts. Why not?

The most important reason has to do with the strength of interest groups in developed democracies and what political scientists call "path dependencies," a tendency to keep social programs moving along a path set by previous policies.[14] In developed countries, long traditions of democratic governance have made representative interest groups and pension policy communities strong. Think of the American Association of Retired Persons and the Social Security Administration in the United States. They are much bigger and more diverse and have greater capacity and resources to resist reforms than their counterparts in developing countries. The United States witnessed the influence of these groups in 2005 when President Bush's reforms met with inexorable pressure from Democrats, pensioners' representatives, and even Republican lawmakers. Radical reforms of all types may simply be less likely in developed democracies. Developed countries tend to favor incremental rather than radical change. Reforms must take account of the interest groups associated with previous policies and are often constrained by what those interest groups will accept. Furthermore, democratic processes in developed countries provide more opportunities for citizens to affect the policy process than in authoritarian regimes or new democracies.

The failure of President Bush's proposed reforms shows that the privatization of Social Security faces particular challenges in the United States. Since the U.S. Social Security program is relatively small, any cuts push American retirees into greater income insecurity. It may be possible to strengthen Social Security with a variety of reforms, but carving out the program seems not only unlikely but unwise.

MAKING WORKPLACE PENSIONS MANDATORY

While only two developed countries have cut back Social Security to introduce individual accounts, a growing number of developed countries have supplemented their Social Security programs by making pre-existing workplace pension systems mandatory or quasi-mandatory. This approach was taken by the Netherlands starting in 1947, Switzerland in the 1960s, and Australia and Denmark in the 1990s. New Zealand introduced its "KiwiSaver" program in 2007, which inspired the United Kingdom to consider similar reforms in 2008.[15] The experiences of English-speaking countries such as Australia, New Zealand, and the United

Kingdom are the most relevant examples for the United States to emulate since these countries share a similar cultural heritage, reflected in a lesser reliance on the state and a greater trust in market provision.

Countries that have made their workplace pension systems mandatory or quasi-mandatory share certain characteristics. They tend to have smaller Social Security programs that pay lower benefits—creating a need for additional retirement income. Social Security in the United States, for instance, replaces only 40% of pre-retirement income on average, meaning that most people require additional income in old age. This compares to a 60–70% replacement rate for Social Security in continental European countries such as France, Germany, Italy, and Spain.

Countries that have opted for mandatory employer pensions also have preexisting voluntary workplace pension systems covering between 15% and 50% of the population. These voluntary systems cover primarily state employees and white-collar workers. In making their workplace pension systems mandatory, these countries have often allowed employers with more generous existing workplace pension schemes to maintain those schemes. Any new contributions for employers and/or employees not previously covered are phased in over time.

The Netherlands was the pioneer in mandating workplace pensions, starting in 1947, and has long been an exceptional case in Europe. Switzerland mandated workplace pensions after a 1972 referendum. The Swiss reform began as a move by insurers and conservative politicians to prevent the formerly communist Labor Party from expanding the Social Security-based pension system.[16] Denmark moved toward mandatory workplace pensions in 1991 in an effort to provide adequate pensions for blue-collar workers. Eighty-two percent of Danes now are covered by a workplace pension.[17] Until recently, the Dutch, Danish, and Swiss models were seen as outliers to the European norms since these countries had smaller Social Security programs. However, a growing number of European and other countries have adopted this approach to pension reform.

In addition to the European models of mandatory workplace pensions, Australia's 1992 pension reform has provided an influential global model. The timing of Australia's new pension system coincided with the global trend toward pension privatization. Its design had a distinctly promarket flavor that took inspiration from the Chilean model. The idea to mandate workplace pensions in Australia came out of negotiations between employers and trade unions. Trade unions wanted better pensions for workers and in 1986 agreed to accept lower wage increases in exchange for a workplace pension system funded by a 3% employer contribution. In 1992, the Australian government made this system mandatory and increased the contribution amount from 3% in 1992 to 7% in 2001 and 9% starting in 2002. Employers with better pension schemes can opt out of the system. Eighty-nine percent of all Australian workers are enrolled in a workplace pension. Workplace pensions in Australia are very lightly regulated, with no guaranteed returns and a wide variety of funds offering a range of products with little government control. Administrative fees are high. Pension funds are levied for contributions as well as investment returns and withdrawals — making Australia the only country in the world to have triple taxation. The Australian government is currently reviewing the tax situation, contribution amount, and regulation of its so-called superannuation funds. Between 1990 and 2002, the superannuation funds experienced high returns of approximately 8% per annum, ensuring the popularity of the program. It remains to be seen how lower returns may impact the system.

New Zealand passed its KiwiSaver pension system in 2006 and implemented it starting in 2007. Like Australia, New Zealand has a small state retirement pension paid for entirely by general tax revenues (rather than a special payroll tax contribution, as in the United States and most other countries). Anyone who meets residency requirements is eligible to receive the state pension. Given the relatively small amount of the benefits, however, many New Zealanders need a more generous supplemental pension. Nonetheless, only 15% of employees were enrolled in a workplace pension system. This provided the impetus for the KiwiSaver program. Since 2007, all new employees are automatically enrolled in a KiwiSaver account to which they contribute 4% of earnings. Their investments are channeled to a default pension investment fund unless they select another option. Employees have eight weeks to opt out of the system. They may also choose to increase their contribution rate to up to 8%. New enrollees receive a government subsidy of 1,000 New Zealand dollars when they open their account. Employers may also contribute to the accounts and receive a tax break on contributions of up to 4% of salary. The New Zealand reform is unique in not requiring employer contributions as well as in making enrollment automatic but optional.[18]

KiwiSaver proved inspirational in the United Kingdom, where successive Labor governments sought to re-reform the pension system after Thatcher's 1986 reforms. The United Kingdom, like the United States, provides a low level of Social Security benefits, which has become increasingly insufficient as the population ages. A 2007 law increased protection for poorer pensioners while creating new opportunities for pension savings. In 2008, the government proposed a new employer-based pension savings system that drew upon the KiwiSaver model of mandatory enrollment with an option for employees to opt out. It proposed a mandatory contribution of 8% of earnings between 5,035 and 33,540 pounds (up to a maximum of 3,600 pounds per year). Employers would pay at least 3% of the required contribution with the rest to be paid by employees (and by the government through tax breaks). Contributions would be phased in over time through the national tax system. Pension savings accounts would be easily portable, and a great deal of emphasis was placed on fair regulation given the mis-selling of the Thatcher-era funds. Employers with existing workplace pensions could maintain their current scheme if a straightforward test found it more generous. The government would work with the pension industry to design pension savings funds, impose strict limits on fees, and ensure low costs.

Australia, New Zealand, and the United Kingdom have made major strides toward making pension savings mandatory for all. The experiences of these countries are particularly relevant to the United States because of cultural and pension system similarities.

LESSONS FOR U.S. PENSION REFORM

What should the United States learn from these international experiences? This brief review suggests four lessons. The first lesson is that the route to reform in developed countries is becoming increasingly clear. Carving out Social Security to divert contributions to individual pension savings accounts is neither wise nor feasible. This approach has failed in the United States and in most other developed countries. Except in extreme cases, political interest groups are too strong to bring about Social Security cuts. Moreover, privatization does not address the key problem of Social Security reform—ensuring adequate benefits. While carve-outs have stalled in developed countries worldwide, a growing number of advanced industrial countries have introduced pension savings accounts for all by making enrollment in a workplace pension mandatory or quasi-mandatory. This is the most promising way forward for U.S. reform. It is a route increasingly taken by English-speaking countries like the United States with small Social Security programs.

The second lesson is that, in requiring a workplace pension for all, governments have in effect designed and introduced a new mandatory or quasi-mandatory workplace pension system while allowing successful employer pension schemes to carry on untouched. This approach enables governments to correct design flaws in the existing workplace pension system without destroying employer plans that already function effectively. Only ineffective employer programs are replaced, which enhances the political legitimacy of the reforms.

A third lesson is that any new mandatory pension contributions can be phased in over time. Reducing the immediate economic effect on employers and employees makes the introduction of a new system more politically feasible.

A fourth lesson is that no two reforms are exactly alike. While the Australia, New Zealand, and proposed United Kingdom models share a host of similarities, they also differ in a variety of ways that reflect the conditions in those countries and the nature of their domestic political debates. Should the United States take this route to reform, it faces a number of important pension system design decisions, including:

- Should employee contributions be mandatory, or should individuals be allowed to opt out?
- Should employer contributions be mandatory?
- Should there be tax breaks for employee and/or employer contributions?
- Should contributions be invested in a default fund?
- How would a default fund be regulated and managed?
- Should pension funds be required to provide a guaranteed rate of return?
- How should withdrawals be handled?
- Can regulation of existing workplace pension schemes be improved at the same time?
- Should tax-free contribution limits be reduced to pay for new entrants?

These design choices are discussed in the following sections.

RAISING AWARENESS OF THE NEED
FOR U.S. PENSION REFORM

A first step for pension reform in the United States is to explain to people that the current 401(k)-based workplace pension system has serious problems. Public awareness of workplace pension failures is not as high as the awareness of Social Security's ills. Any reform must begin by focusing popular attention on workplace pension issues, which are particularly salient since the financial market crisis beginning in 2008.

While employers have moved away from defined benefit pension systems, which provided generous pensions to employees with long tenures at large firms, contributory workplace pension systems have shown very poor results in terms of creating an adequate retirement income for most Americans. People do not contribute enough to their individual pension savings accounts, called 401(k)s after a clause in the U.S. tax code; they often cash out the balances when they leave their employers; they make bad investment choices, keeping too much in company stock for instance; and they are most likely to make poor decisions at retirement, taking lump-sum payments instead of annuities. As a result, balances in most 401(k) accounts are too low to provide adequate benefits in retirement. The system needs to change now that more Americans are dependent on these accounts.

DESIGNING A NEW U.S. SYSTEM

The U.S. 401(k) system has been reformed multiple times, most recently to enable greater auto-enrollment by employers. However, it has never been fixed. Any new reform needs to grapple with the problem of how to improve the workplace retirement system while addressing the needs of employers, investment companies, and those individuals with balances or business interests in the current system.

One of the critical choices for policymakers concerns whether to make contributions truly mandatory (as in Australia) or to make enrollment mandatory but allow individuals to opt out of making contributions (as in New Zealand). Both approaches have strengths and weaknesses. Making contributions mandatory helps to ensure adequate pensions for all and protects people against saving too little for retirement. However, there are also compelling reasons to allow individuals to opt out of retirement saving. Some individuals may face current issues of insufficient income or extraordinary circumstances. Their immediate concerns need to be balanced against the possibility that employees may be coerced by their employers to opt out, particularly if employer matching contributions are required.

Another crucial design choice in creating a new mandatory workplace system is the question of who will pay. Typically, employers and employees divide the cost of paying for Social Security and workplace pensions. However, it is possible that employers will oppose any reform that requires an employer contribution. One way to address this is to require contributions from employees but leave employer contributions voluntary, although that puts the onus of retirement saving on the worker. It also creates a comparative advantage for employers who do not offer benefits, putting cost pressure on other firms and encouraging them to limit or eliminate pension benefits, particularly for lower-skilled workers. Requiring all employers to contribute would make it less of a handicap to offer pension benefits.

Design of a default fund is another crucial decision. Default options are important because research shows that many employees stay with whatever the default option is in their pension plan rather than face difficult pension savings decisions. A default fund open to millions of new enrollees would set a standard for competing pension savings accounts. One approach would offer a small number of relatively conservative pension savings options. This is the approach taken by the U.S. Thrift Savings Plan, which is offered on a voluntary basis to all federal employees. It limits the likelihood that employees will put all their eggs in one basket or make a seriously bad choice. Another possibility is to automatically enroll individuals in an age-appropriate life-cycle fund that would invest in a mix of stocks and bonds appropriate for a particular age cohort. This further protects individuals from poor investment choices. Another possibility is to require individuals to invest in the funds of a select group of investment companies chosen by the employer — the standard practice in many 401(k) plans today. Yet another possibility is to have the government create a large, low-cost investment fund and contract out its management to a private investment company. This has the advantages of pooling resources and reducing fees. A default pension fund can be designed in many different ways to protect individuals to a greater or lesser degree from the risks of poor investment choices and high management fees.

Another reform design issue is whether the government should guarantee returns in individual pension savings accounts. The government would be mandating contributions so could be seen to share part of the responsibility for guaranteeing returns. Guaranteed returns reduce investment risk on the part of savers at the expense of investment choice and individual opportunity to gain by investment behavior. Again, the question here is whether individuals or the government should bear the risk of retirement insecurity and to what degree.

A further consideration is the way funds may be withdrawn from individual pension savings accounts. While many people choose lump-sum distributions, life annuities provide better protection against the risks of income insecurity. The architects of a mandatory workplace system will have to decide whether to require annuities or make that the default option and allow individuals to select additional options for retirement income.

In creating a new workplace pension system, U.S. policymakers must consider needed changes to existing workplace pension schemes. Existing schemes that meet or exceed the standards of the new system will likely continue to operate. Thus, part of the current system will remain, and policymakers need to decide how to improve it. One way would be to enable participants to invest in the new default fund and force existing funds to compete. Another would be to create new regulation on fund choices, contribution decisions, and income decisions that would make existing funds more compatible with the new standards.

Yet another issue is how to pay for the new system. One option is to transfer tax breaks from the existing workplace pension system. Instead of providing an incentive to invest in a 401(k) account, the government could provide similar incentives to invest in the new accounts. However, because of the larger number of contributors, the size of the individual tax break might have to be lower. This would help new enrollees, who benefit from new tax breaks, but harm the interests of wealthier citizens contributing the maximum to existing accounts. A more serious factor is the extra costs a mandatory system would impose on those employers and employees not currently contributing to an individual retirement account or 401(k) fund. Such costs could be phased in over time but would still amount to a new tax on incomes. Giving individuals the right to opt out would seem to address this issue, but at the expense of failing to make retirement more secure.

	TARGET POPULATION	NATURE OF COMPULSION	NUMBER OF MEMBERS	MINIMUM CONTRIBUTION	BENEFIT RESTRICTION
Chilean AFP (Administradores de Fondos de Pensiones) [1981]	All employees and self-employed	Employee contributions compulsory	Roughly 7.1 million in 2004	10% of the first 22,000 of gross wages paid by employee	Withdrawal available after age 60 for women, 65 for men (as annuity or drawdown)
Australia Superannuation Guarantee [1992]	All employees and self-employed	Employee contributions compulsory	9 million in 2005	9% of gross earnings	Withdrawal available after age 60 (as lump sum, annuity, or mixture)
Sweden Premium Pension [1998]	All employees and self-employed	Employee and employer contributions compulsory	5.3 million in 2004	2.5% of gross earnings (split between employee and employer)	Withdrawal between age 61 and 67 (as annuity)
New Zealand KiwiSaver [2007]	All employees and self-employed	Automatic enrollment with the right to opt out	680,000 after seven years	4% of gross salary/wages	Withdrawal available after age 65 (as lump sum or annuity) or after three years for first-home buyers
United Kingdom National Pensions Savings Scheme (proposal) [2010]	All employees from age 21, with earnings threshold	Automatic enrollment with the right to opt out / Employer contributions compulsory	7 million	5% of gross earnings by employees and 3% by employers	Withdrawal between age 55 and 75 (as annuity or equivalent drawdown)
U.S. 401(k) [1981]	All employees and self-employed	Automatic enrollment permissible subject to employer criteria	45 million in 2001	None	Withdrawal available after age 59.5 until 70.5 (maximum) / Loan provisions
U.S. Thrift Savings Plan [1987]	All federal employees	Automatic enrollment, contribution voluntary	3.5 million in 2004	None	Withdrawal upon retirement (as annuity, partial withdrawal, or transfer)

Sources: Alison O'Connell, "NPSS Policy and Design Choices" (discussion paper, Pensions Policy Institute, April 2006), http://www.pensionspolicyinstitute.org.uk/news.asp?p=218&s=2&a=0; and Organization for Economic Cooperation and Development, "Public Pensions and Retirement Savings," OECD Economic Surveys 2007, no. 8 (April 2007): 67–99.

Table 5.2   Selected mandatory and U.S. voluntary workplace pension systems compared

Reforming the U.S. pension system means choosing the right model and grappling with numerous policy choices. The authors of this book have presented a number of new ideas to improve retirement income security for all Americans. International experiences provide a further set of lessons for policymakers to consider. Table 5.2 gives a comparative overview of current U.S. voluntary systems and mandatory models from around the world.

CONCLUSION

This review of international trends in pension reform suggests that perhaps the most promising way forward for U.S. reform is the route mapped out by the Australians and New Zealanders — making enrollment in a workplace pension mandatory and creating a new pension savings scheme that will prove attractive to both employees and employers. Employers with generous preexisting workplace pension schemes should be enabled to opt out if they can prove that their scheme offers equal or higher benefits.

This approach achieves the promise of benefit adequacy by saving Social Security and mandating workplace pensions for all. Such a reform can be funded by redirecting the tax breaks of the existing workplace pension system, which have increased dramatically in recent years. This is not to say that the United States should slavishly copy the Australian or New Zealand model, but the general approach of supplementing a smaller Social Security program with mandatory workplace pensions may be the most amenable and politically feasible option.

NOTES

1   Mitchell A. Orenstein, *Privatizing Pensions: The Transnational Campaign for Social Security Reform* (Princeton, NJ: Princeton University Press, 2008). See also Katharina Müller, *Privatising Old-Age Security: Latin America and Eastern Europe Compared* (Northampton, MA: Edward Elgar Publishing, 2003).

2   Martin Rein and John Turner, "Public-Private Interactions: Mandatory Pensions in Australia, the Netherlands and Switzerland," *Review of Population and Social Policy* 10 (2001): 107–53. See also Organization for Economic Cooperation and Development, "Public Pensions and Retirement Savings," *OECD Economic Surveys 2007*, no. 8 (April 2007): 67–99.

3   One prominent work advocating individual pension savings accounts is World Bank, *Averting the Old Age Crisis: Policies to Protect the Old and Promote Growth* (Oxford: Oxford University Press, 1994). See also Martin Feldstein, "Structural Reform of Social Security," *Journal of Economic Perspectives* 19, no. 2 (2005): 33–55.

4   For a full account, see Sarah M. Brooks, "Interdependent and Domestic Foundations of Policy Change: The Diffusion of Pension Privatization Around the World," *International Studies Quarterly* 49, no. 2 (2005): 273–94.

5   Orenstein, *Privatizing Pensions*.

6   Juan Gabriel Valdes, *Pinochet's Economists: The Chicago School in Chile* (Cambridge: Cambridge University Press, 1995).

7   Müller, *Privatising Old-Age Security.*

8   Sarah M. Brooks, "International Financial Institutions and the Diffusion of Foreign Models for Social Security Reform in Latin America," in *Learning from Foreign Models in Latin American Policy Reform,* ed. Kurt Weyland (Washington, DC: Woodrow Wilson Center Press; Baltimore: Johns Hopkins University Press, 2004), chap. 3.

9   David Snelbecker, "Pension Reform in Eastern Europe and Eurasia: Experiences and Lessons Learned" (prepared for USAID Workshop for Practitioners on Tax and Pension Reform, Washington, DC, June 27–29, 2005).

10 Gustavo Demarco, "The Argentine Pension System Reform and International Lessons," in *Learning from Foreign Models in Latin American Policy Reform,* ed. Kurt Weyland (Washington, DC: Woodrow Wilson Center Press; Baltimore: Johns Hopkins University Press, 2004), chap. 4.

11 Republic of South Africa National Treasury, "Social Security and Retirement Reform: Second Discussion Paper" (discussion paper, Republic of South Africa National Treasury, February 2007).

12 David Blake, "Two Decades of Pension Reform in the UK: What are the Implications for Occupational Pension Schemes," *Employee Relations* 22, no. 3 (2000): 223.

13 Sweden spends approximately 7.4% of its gross domestic product (GDP) on pensions compared to 4.4% in the United States.

14 Paul Pierson, "When Effect Becomes Cause: Policy Feedback and Political Change," *World Politics* 45, no. 4 (July 1993): 595–628.

15 OECD, "Public Pensions and Retirement Savings." For pension reform in the United Kingdom, see UK Department for Work and Pensions, "Pensions Reform — 2010 Onwards," http://www.dwp.gov.uk/pensionsreform/.

16 Rein and Turner, "Public-Private Interactions," 107–53; and Matthieu Leimgruber, *Solidarity without the State?: Business and the Shaping of the Swiss Welfare State, 1890–2000* (Cambridge: Cambridge University Press, 2008), chap. 4.

17 Christoffer Green-Pedersen and Anders Lindbom, "Politics within Paths: Trajectories of Danish and Swedish Earnings-Related Pensions," *Journal of European Social Policy* 16, no. 3 (August 2006): 245–58.

18 OECD, "Public Pensions and Retirement Savings." Also, Eric Toder and Surachai Khitatrakun, "Final Report to Inland Revenue," *KiwiSaver Evaluation Literature Review* (Tax Policy Center, December 4, 2006), http://www.urban.org/url.cfm?ID=411400.

Contributors

GARY BURTLESS is John C. and Nancy D. Whitehead Chair in Economic Studies at The Brookings Institution in Washington, DC. He has published numerous influential books and articles on a wide variety of economic and social policy issues, including aging, social insurance, income distribution, and labor markets.

TERESA GHILARDUCCI is Irene and Bernard L. Schwartz Professor of Economic Policy Analysis at the New School for Social Research. She is the author of *When I'm Sixty-Four: The Plot against Pensions and the Plan to Save Them* (Princeton, NJ: Princeton University Press, 2008).

ALICIA H. MUNNELL is Peter F. Drucker Professor of Management Sciences at the Carroll School of Management and director of the Center for Retirement Research at Boston College. She is the author, with Steven Sass, of *Working Longer: The Solution to the Retirement Income Challenge* (Washington, DC: Brookings Institution Press, 2008).

MITCHELL A. ORENSTEIN is S. Richard Hirsch Associate Professor of European Studies at Johns Hopkins University, Paul H. Nitze School of Advanced International Studies in Washington, DC. He is the author of *Privatizing Pensions: The Transnational Campaign for Social Security Reform* (Princeton, NJ: Princeton University Press, 2008).